Praise for *The Good Boss*

"*The Good Boss* is a much-needed look into the powerful role a good boss can play in shaping the future workforce, full of relatable stories that felt all too familiar at times! My career wouldn't be where it is without my bosses supporting me along the way, and this book will help create more good bosses for the next wave of high potential women."

—Kelly Campbell Kotzman, president of Hulu

"*The Good Boss* frames the full scope of challenges that women encounter. The book is a must-read for every male CEO and manager, and it gives all of us practical ways we can support women every day."

—Brian Grey, CEO of Remind and former CEO of The Bleacher Report

"Kate is one of the most graceful leaders and bosses I know. I can't think of a better person to lead us forward. I so wish I'd had this book, and that my bosses had had it as well—and that it could have taught me how to choose empowering bosses."

—Candice Carpenter Olson, founder of iVillage

"*The Good Boss* reminds us that a strong leader is a leader for everyone, and all managers—men and women alike—have a part to play in supporting the women who work for them."

—Cara Shortsleeve, CEO of The Leadership Consortium

"Any leader recognizes the critical importance of a high-performing team. *The Good Boss* provides an understanding of why diverse organizations outperform their peers and actionable guidance on how to get there."

—Laurence Franklin, former CEO of Tumi

"Finally, a practical guide for supporting and empowering women in the workplace, from someone who has been doing it for years. "
—Kristen Chase, CEO and cofounder of Cool Mom Picks

"*The Good Boss* helps managers genuinely understand, support, and develop the women on their teams. A must-read for leaders who are serious about helping people reach their full potential."
—Robert Avossa, EdD, national education leader

"I look back on my career and realize how much easier it would have been had I had more good bosses. This book should encourage all women to seek to work in organizations where they can be mentored by good bosses—it is critically important."
—Deborah Quazzo, managing partner of GSV Ventures and cofounder of ASU+GSV Summit

"With rich stories and practical, real-world scenarios that we can *all* follow, *The Good Boss* helps us all, from the workplace veteran struggling against antiquated norms to the new mom to the boss struggling to help in each situation. *The Good Boss* should be required reading for all of us—to not only understand the potential landmines, but also how to navigate them with absolute aplomb."
—Darria Long, MD, national bestselling author of *Mom Hacks* and international medical TV contributor

"Managers need practical advice for how to be authentic leaders, and *The Good Boss* offers up real-world scenarios and natural approaches to manage challenging situations. Every manager should have it on their shelves."
—Stephen Bailey, CEO/founder of ExecOnline

THE
GOOD
BOSS

THE
GOOD
BOSS

Nine Ways Every Manager Can
Support Women at Work

Kate Eberle Walker

BenBella Books, Inc.
Dallas, TX

BenBella Books, Inc.
10440 N. Central Expressway
Suite 800
BenBella Dallas, TX 75231
www.benbellabooks.com
Send feedback to feedback@benbellabooks.com

BenBella is a federally registered trademark.

Printed in the United States of America
10 9 8 7 6 5 4 3 2 1

Library of Congress Cataloging-in-Publication Data: 2020949207
ISBN 9781950665815 (trade cloth)
ISBN 9781953295163 (electronic)

Editing by Claire Schulz
Copyediting by Michael Fedison
Proofreading by Christine Florie and Chris Gage
Indexing by WordCo Indexing Services, Inc.
Text design and composition by Aaron Edmiston
Cover design by Oceana Garceau
Cover photo © iStock / kentarcajuan
Printed by Lake Book Manufacturing

Distributed to the trade by Two Rivers Distribution, an Ingram brand
www.tworiversdistribution.com

Dedicated to my father, Robert F. Eberle Jr.,
who was a good boss to many women, and set the
standard for what I expected from my own bosses.

CONTENTS

INTRODUCTION

recently caught up over lunch with my friend Matt, a guy I worked with at my first job out of college, in investment banking at Goldman Sachs. As we sat and sipped lattes after our meal, it sparked a memory of the coffee breaks I used to take with my fellow female bankers. I started reminiscing about all the things we carefully navigated back then, making sure that we did or said the right thing, just to get a chance to be taken seriously.

It had been twenty years since we began navigating our professional lives. Especially in those early years, I had relied heavily on the women I worked with to pool and share our collective intelligence on how to successfully interact at work. I told Matt about how, whenever someone got assigned to a new manager, we would all pitch in with what we knew, or had heard, about him:[*,1]

"Be careful not to speak in the meeting unless he asks you a question."

"He won't respect you unless you speak up."

"Don't correct him in front of other people even if you know his numbers are wrong."

"Make sure he thinks your ideas are actually his."

"He will double-check everything you do. Don't take it personally."

"Try to blend in at his client meetings: don't wear a skirt."

"Try to stand out at his client meetings: make sure you wear a skirt."

"Don't go into his office alone."

---

* The vast majority of our managers were "him," not "her." As of 2019, less than 17 percent of senior leaders in US investment banking were women. I can only assume it was far less than that back in 1998; financial firms didn't report publicly on female management representation until well into the 2000s.

Now, decades later, I marveled to Matt about how much time we spent figuring that stuff out. I had outgrown it only by making it to a point in my career where I got to set the tone, instead of spending my energy anticipating and adapting to what others wanted me to do. But, I continued, these challenges still exist for women working their way up, and, like me, these women will succeed only if they put energy and effort into figuring out how to accommodate the expectations that others have for them. I looked across the café table at Matt and I realized that my former colleague was staring at me blankly. None of what I was talking about rang familiar to him.

"Wait," I asked, "didn't you guys worry about any of that stuff?"

"I don't know." He shrugged. "I guess we just focused on the work."

Same Game, Different Odds

In the workplace, the path for women has more friction and requires more effort than the equivalent path for men. It's like in the game Chutes and Ladders. Every player has the same goal: to get from the starting square (1) to the top square (100). As you move along the game board, you encounter ladders that propel you ahead, and chutes that set you back. The average number of turns it takes for a player to reach the top is 39.2.[2] But it can be done in as few as seven spins, or it can require a far greater number of spins and steps.*

In a board game, every player's odds are equal.† In the working world, however, the odds are anything but. For every one hundred

---

* If you are a math nerd like me, you may be interested to know that there is an abundance of resources that have run statistical analyses on the odds of success in Chutes and Ladders using Markov chains.

† Well, almost equal. Again, for the benefit of the math nerds, if you go first, you have a slightly higher chance, 50.9 percent, of winning the game, according to statistician Karl Broman on his blog.

men promoted to the manager level, only seventy-two women will be promoted.[3] Applying the dynamics of today's working environment to a game of Chutes and Ladders, men have a far greater chance of getting the straight upward path. They are more likely to land on square 28, the one that gets you on the long straight ladder that advances you fifty-six squares in a single turn.

Women, on the other hand, get a mix of short ladders and chutes on their path. "Even among men and women identified as having high potential from the start, women are less likely to get the 'hot jobs' that are springboards to bigger roles," says a 2019 *Wall Street Journal* report.[4] In the language of Chutes and Ladders, they are more likely to land on square 9. That's the one with the ladder that seems pretty good because it moves you up twenty-two squares, but actually it's doing you a disservice because it skips you over square 28, leaving you no opportunity to catch the big ladder all the way up to the top.

The Work of Navigating a Workplace Not Built for Women

Society has started to acknowledge the double load that women carry at work and at home, holding all the duties that come with their job, plus bearing primary responsibility for household management. But there is another double load that weighs on women entirely within the workplace. Women not only need to do their actual work but they also need to think about how they are being perceived as they are doing it. They have to think about how to do it in the right way, the way that will be best received, the way that won't seem too aggressive or too weak. While men are just focusing on doing their jobs, women are figuring out a series of strategies to deploy just to make sure that their work will be accepted. It's exhausting.

When I first started writing advice for women on how to succeed in the workplace, I set out to find some collective wisdom among successful women. What could we teach young women today about how to navigate all these pitfalls? I wanted to hear the stories of brilliant tactics, or shortcut solutions, that had gotten these women ahead. The times they had negotiated a good job offer into a great one. The times they had successfully advocated for their own promotions.

There was a fatal flaw in my approach. I was stuck in the mindset that women needed to learn how to adapt themselves to their environment to be successful. I was trying to change the way the women played the game, to find a smarter way for them to spin the wheel, so that they could land on the right squares on the board. What I needed to do instead was ask how we could change the game.

It turns out that when I interviewed women to collect their strategies for success, these undeniably successful women weren't able to rattle off an impressive list of things they had done. Instead, they said things like:

"I've actually never asked for a raise," or,

"My biggest opportunities kind of just came to me."

But I did find a common thread. As I sorted through the stories these women shared with me, each was actually a story about a good boss. Someone who had promoted her, encouraged her, and given her raises and opportunities before she ever had to ask for them. The managers of these women had accelerated their paths by taking some of the obstacles out of the way. These women hadn't wasted a lot of emotional energy figuring out how to ask for opportunities. They were good at their jobs, their bosses recognized that, and the opportunities followed.

Good Bosses Make the Difference

This shouldn't have been a surprise, because the same was true for me. In my first several years out of business school, I advanced rapidly. I got significant raises at least once a year, along with promotions. All of this was offered to me by my boss; he saw that I was talented and ambitious, and he rewarded me for it. He knew that the company benefited from the value I created. Those raises and promotions also made me loyal; not once did I think about leaving my job. Then that boss left the company. My job remained the same but under new management. The promotions, opportunities, and raises that I had enjoyed in the early years of my career stopped coming my way.

It was in this context that a mutual acquaintance introduced me to Mandy Ginsberg, the then CEO of Tutor.com. Our first conversation flowed easily. We both shared a big ambition and vision for building a great education company. She listened to me in a way that none of my previous bosses ever had. Twenty minutes into that first conversation, she said, "I think you should come work with me." So I did.

I joined her at Tutor.com, and together we went on to acquire The Princeton Review, one of the biggest brands in consumer education, with Mandy as CEO. With her own career path taking her forward to the CEO role at Match Group, she designated me as her successor. In late 2015, at age thirty-nine, I became the CEO of The Princeton Review.

I didn't break into the C-suite, or even contemplate the possibility, until I went to work for a boss who saw me as a CEO. This is typical for women leaders. Of the women who have been CEOs of Fortune 1000 companies, 65 percent say that they didn't realize they had the potential to become a CEO until someone else, typically a boss or mentor, told them.[5]

My experiences have shown that people tend to hire those who fit the models of success that they have already seen. In many cases, this means hiring people who are like themselves. Because of this dynamic, hiring and promoting women has rested disproportionately on the shoulders of other women. As a female CEO, when you reach the top of your organization, you look to "pay it forward" by helping other women get there too.

"Women of my generation got to the C-suite because of other women bosses. That thing people say, that women tear each other down, and don't help each other, has rarely been true in my experience. Many of us have gotten here because of great female leaders who helped us. In turn we continue to believe in women supporting each other, and when we become the leaders, we take more women with us. But we need to make it a universal boss thing, not a 'woman thing,'" says Shannon, the CEO of a hospitality company.

Not Every Manager of a Woman Can, or Should, Be a Woman

We can't leave it only to women to hire more women, to people of color to hire more people of color, and so forth. Everyone needs to deliberately and actively seek to place more diverse representation in leadership roles.

Many women have learned the difficult lesson that just being good at your job isn't enough to become successful. But we've also learned an equally powerful and positive lesson: being good at your job, *and* having someone with more power than you recognize it and support you, is enough. Until society catches up with women, talented women need good bosses to help them succeed. Many of those good bosses for women will be men.

We do need to give women strong female role models. But no one ever said that those role models also have to be their direct managers. So, if you're a male manager, and you've scanned this book up until now thinking, "Well, I can't be a female role model, so this doesn't help me," it's time to tune back in.

You know how important your own boss is to your day-to-day life and your career trajectory. A good boss makes all the difference. They heavily influence how you feel about your work, how you are perceived by others in the organization, and which opportunities you are given. Whoever you are, you can be that good boss for the women who work for you. A good boss can catapult a woman forward, and the wrong boss can keep her from ever having a chance to advance. To help women succeed in the workplace, we need to place responsibility with their managers.

Male Managers Need to Be Part of the Solution

Ask any woman about her boss, and chances are it will be a man. Men fill two-thirds of mid-management roles in the Fortune 500, and this number rises higher with every management level.[6] Managers are responsible for developing and supporting future women leaders, and the majority of those managers are men.

Yet too often the conversation about how to be a good boss for women centers on female bosses. The first three results from a Google search I did for "how to be a good boss for women" were:

7 Girl Bosses Share Their Best Career Advice
10 Female Leaders on How to Be a Good Manager
5 Mistakes Women Bosses Make

Nowhere on the entire first page of search results was there any advice addressed to men. This implication, that "women helping women" is the way forward for women in the workplace, is flawed when the problem we are trying to solve is that there are not enough women in senior roles. Only 7.6 percent of Fortune 500 CEOs, and 21 percent of all C-suite executives, are women.[7] There aren't enough women to help all the women we want to elevate to success in the future. If we rely on only women to pull up the next generation, women will remain stuck below their full potential for years to come. I was lucky enough to find a female CEO to mentor and develop me. But Mandy wasn't a great boss because she was a woman. Everything she did to help me was something a man could have done too. Male managers need to work for equality in the workforce as well. We need men need to be part of the solution.

I've spent a lot of time with men in the workplace. Across all of the conversations I've had with male managers—my bosses, my fellow CEOs, managers who work for me, and those who don't work for me but are willing to listen to my advice—one thing that I will say with confidence is that the vast majority of these men have good intentions. They genuinely want to support women on their teams and to help more women advance to leadership positions. They mean well but they don't always get it right. "I'm 100 percent in favor of supporting women in my company," a male CEO confided to me, "but I'm not always sure what the right thing to do is."

It's not that men don't want to make things better; it's that they don't exactly know how to. You could fill many bookshelves with titles about how men and women differ in their approach to relationships (think *Men Are from Mars, Women Are from Venus*). The workplace is driven by relationships, too, and though we've read a lot of headlines in the past few years about how often lines are blurred between romantic and professional relationships, the reality is that the vast majority of workplace relationships are platonic. And the most important ones are between managers and the people who report to them.

How *The Good Boss* Works

A lot of what this book will cover are the seemingly little things that chip away at a woman's work experience. Nuances and subtleties that may seem inconsequential in isolation, but when they happen again and again, they build up and create a weight. When you take the time to learn the perspective of women and to implement simple strategies for supporting them, it can add up to a fundamental shift in the work environment for women.

There are some things, many things in fact, that are beyond your control as a manager. This book is about doing what you can as a manager to have a meaningful impact on the day-to-day experience of the women who work for you. To do this in a realistic way, we also need to acknowledge what you can't do. You can be a great manager for every person who works for you, but you can't be the perfect role model for each of them. Companies need to provide that. It's the job of company leadership, the board and the executives, to ensure that there are diverse representative role models at the top of the organization.

This book is for all managers of women, whether managing one, one hundred, or one thousand employees. It includes the female managers who want to continue to support women in the future amid evolving expectations of the workplace and generational shifts in what women expect from their employers. It is for the well-intentioned male managers who want to support women, and who want some approachable advice on how to do it. There's also a lot in here for professional women looking for insight on what to expect from your manager, with an appendix entirely dedicated to advice on how to find your good boss.

The good news is that many of the things you can do to support women are not that hard. This book offers up nine rules, each centered on one practical thing that managers can do to be better bosses for women. Each chapter will cover three recurring elements: perspective on a woman's experience, recommendations for better ways to do things, and a vision for structural changes with broad, lasting impact.

Perspective: What Does Today's Workplace Feel Like for Women?

Each section will begin with some insight into what happens to women in common workplace contexts. These are stories, told by women, about their experiences. The goal of sharing these stories is to give you perspective, understanding, and empathy. This is what she actually experiences, and this is how she feels about it. Having that awareness of the things that you and others say and do, and the impact they have, is the first step.

A Better Way: Strategies for Easing Her Path

With the improved understanding of a woman's experience at work, we will go on to identify better ways for managers to handle situations to give more support to the women who work for them. Many of these examples involve simple changes you can make to your own words and actions, or new approaches and questions you can use in your conversations as a manager. Small changes can go a surprisingly long way. Do these simple things well, and you individually can become a good boss for women.

Vision for Structural Improvement: Changes to Drive Broad, Lasting Impact

A central theme of this book is that change can happen in small increments; every manager can make a difference. But bigger impact, at the organizational level, is important, too, and makes the work of women and their managers much easier. CEOs spend a lot of time thinking about ways to ensure diversity and balanced representation across their companies. Many are implementing systems and programs that have changed the dynamic for women at their company. Each chapter ends with a high-impact idea that has been put into action inside one or more companies, to showcase the bigger changes that can jump us further down the path to equality in the workplace.

How to Read the Rules

Each rule stands alone, so if one of them catches your eye and you want to go there first, by all means, go for it. They don't need to be read in order. Think of it like listening to an album; I've ordered them as I think they play best, but if you feel like jumping ahead to a song in the middle, you won't get lost. The rules are ordered to roughly follow the progression of an average woman's career experience—that is, more often than not, marriage comes before babies. But I'm not a traditionalist about these things. When there's a helpful connection to be made between one rule and another, I'll call it out and cross-reference you there.

All these rules are relevant and applicable to all women and all managers. This is not a case of reading through and selecting the one that fits you best. They are not mutually exclusive, and there is no quiz at the end to help you identify your "type," as in, "I'm a Rule #5 Boss." In fact, I would love for you to follow all the rules. That said, depending on your style and that of the women who work for you, you may really latch on to some rules more than others and feel that they are most actionable for you. That's great. If you come away from this feeling like you can immediately put Rules #3, 4, and 8 to work in a big way, and keep the others in the back of your mind for context and future reference, then this book will have accomplished what it set out to do. You'll have a deeper understanding of the mindset of women at work, and a framework for how to act differently to improve their experiences. And we'll start with the most basic rule of all: Call Her by Her Name.

RULE #1

CALL HER BY HER NAME

was leading the negotiations of a potential deal to purchase a company. I was the CEO in charge of the deal and forty-one years old at the time. I'd had many conversations with the owner of the business, and we were getting close. The key, he told me, was getting John, one of his "most trusted advisors," on board. John, he said, would be coming to New York the following Wednesday and would be available for an 11 AM meeting in our offices.

"Great," I had said. "Let's do it."

The following Wednesday at 11 AM, I was ready to meet. Another director-level employee, Sean, was working on the deal with me, so he joined the meeting too. The two of us sat along one side of the table waiting for John to arrive. He was running about twenty minutes late, which we laughed about only because he had been so specific about the 11 AM time slot a full week in advance.*

John arrived and took the seat at the head of the conference table, leaning back with one arm stretched out in one direction and his legs sprawled out in the other. It reminded me of something I had learned in my negotiating class at business school about taking up physical space to appear dominant in the conversation.

I kicked off the official meeting but didn't get very far. What I intended to say was, "Thank you for making the trip, John, and for sending your questions over to us. There was a lot in your email that I think we can cover really well today, so my hope is that we'll leave here with you getting the clarity on the deal that you need."

I got as far as "There was a lot . . ." when he began to talk over me.

---

* It turned out John's tardiness was fully justified. There had been a fire in the parking garage of his hotel, and none of the guests, including him, were able to access their cars. John was a self-professed "car guy," and the car in question was a Porsche, so you can imagine his unhappiness as he speculated about what condition it might be in when he did get to it.

"OK," he said, "why don't we start with introductions. I like to get to know people before jumping into the nitty-gritty." He proceeded to tell us about his extensive experience as a private equity investor. "I've done over a hundred deals in my career," he proclaimed, "so I know all about how they go and what to watch out for."

"This will be a really easy conversation then," I interjected, "because I've also done over a hundred deals, so we've both been through this before. I think we can talk really efficiently about the terms and figure out where we need to come together." I wasn't sure if he heard me, because he didn't react or respond to what I said.

Instead of addressing me, he gestured to Sean and prompted him to share his background. Because John had shared a lot of details about his own history, Sean did the same, starting with where he went to college and going through every job he'd had since then.

After Sean finished, John turned to me and asked, "And what about you, young lady?"

I was completely thrown off. *Young lady?* Sean and I exchanged confused looks; I wasn't sure if John even registered that I was the decision maker in the room, but I shrugged and on we trudged. There were multiple disrespectful things that John did in that conversation, but the one that really stung was the use of those two words—"young lady." After that, I was so mad for the rest of the time, absolutely steaming. With that phrase, he conveyed a condescending lack of respect for me and my place in the meeting. Here I was, at the top of my organization, and yet I still could be reduced to insignificance by two words.

I couldn't get past it. John may have won the moment in assuming dominance of the conversation, but in the long run, he hurt himself and his client. Getting a deal done requires a lot of effort and persistence to work things through and keep everyone moving in the same direction. After that meeting with John, I disengaged from the deal and stopped trying to make it happen. I just didn't want to interact with him. Ultimately, the deal fell through.

> "Women clearly aren't happy to be called by anything other than their name."
>
> **OnePoll, 2010 study on the use of names in the workplace**

Women in the workplace just want to be called by their names. This is an essential rule for managers: call her by her name. As obvious as it sounds, there are many nuances to keep in mind. I've boiled them down to four key guidelines.

Beginner Level: Don't Use Terms of Endearment

That means no "dear," no "sweetheart." No "young lady." This one should be a given, but you'd be surprised. A survey by research firm Hiscox found that 41 percent of managers think it's OK to use terms of endearment at work.[1] Yet in a 2010 study by market research site OnePoll, researchers found that 75 percent of women think it's unacceptable to use terms of endearment at work, and 25 percent have felt angry about it at some point.[2]

Terms of endearment are problematic for a few reasons. For one, they are expressly defined by the United States Equal Employment Opportunity Commission as a form of sexual harassment. The US Department of the Interior Office of Civil Rights includes the following on its list of "Examples of Sexual Harassment":

*Terms of endearment, such as calling a co-worker "honey,"
"dear," "sweetheart," or some similar expression. (The
effect is the primary issue rather than intent. Even if the
person "means nothing to you" or you have "used the term
for years" you should be aware that such expressions are
inappropriate.)*

Regardless of whether intended to be affectionate or friendly, terms of endearment come off as condescending, disrespectful, and diminishing. It's easy to steer clear of this land mine as a manager; unlike much of the advice to come in this book, in this case there is no need for nuance or judgment. Just never do it. Don't use terms of endearment with your direct reports or other colleagues. It's probably unwelcome, and likely to make her upset. It's a chronic problem, and according to the OnePoll study, men do it to women far more often than the reverse. Despite it being viewed as a somewhat old-fashioned problem, it continues to plague many men.

President Barack Obama notably apologized during his 2008 presidential campaign for his use of a term of endearment to address a female reporter. In May 2008, at a campaign stop in Detroit, reporter Peggy Agar asked Obama, "Senator, how are you going to help the American autoworkers?"

Obama responded, "Hold on one second, sweetie. We're going to do—we'll do a press avail" (which is a formal question-and-answer session for the reporters on the campaign trail).

Agar, a television reporter for ABC's Detroit affiliate, ended her on-air segment that evening by saying, "This sweetie never got an answer to that question," as footage rolled of Obama walking away from her. The incident created quite a dustup, and Obama called Agar personally a few hours after making the comment. He left her a voice mail in which he apologized, both for not answering her question and for calling her "sweetie."

"That's a bad habit of mine," Obama said in the message. "I do it sometimes with all kinds of people. I mean no disrespect and so I am duly chastened on that front."[3]

As a manager it's your responsibility not only to avoid using these terms yourself but to teach others not to do it. Recognize that it doesn't matter what the background or intentions are of the person using the term. What matters is the impact. Try to speak up about this so that she doesn't have to be the one complaining. With a peer, this can often be done quickly and easily in the moment. If you hear a "dear" or "sweetheart" getting thrown around, a quick "Joe, stick to actual names or I'm going to have to start calling you honey bear" usually does the trick.

If it's a superior saying it rather than your peer, it can be a lot harder to speak up. If you feel comfortable following the above formula, calling it out in the moment is always best. If you don't feel comfortable speaking up, acknowledge the moment with her after the fact; let her know that you heard it and you recognized that it was not OK. It is demoralizing for her when you pretend it didn't happen, or when you try to minimize it, by telling her that he's just old-fashioned, or that he didn't mean anything by it. You can be honest with her that you didn't feel like you could speak up, but you should also apologize that you didn't. (See more on these strategies in Rule #6: Speak Up So That She Doesn't Have To.)

A female executive recently shared a Slack exchange she had with the IT professional at her company. Her laptop was acting up, so she sent him a message to ask for help.

She wrote: "My computer is insanely slow and is constantly crashing. Can you help?"

He responded, "We'll get that fixed, my dear."

When she went to his boss about it, the manager was initially dismissive, minimizing it by explaining that the IT guy was young and probably just didn't understand how to speak appropriately in the workplace. But it is that manager's job to teach his direct report what's appropriate. The IT professional needed to be told, "Don't say 'my dear,'" and he needed to be taught what is acceptable. His manager eventually did give him the feedback directly and simply, and suggested that he could instead say "my friend" if his goal is to convey a friendly tone. Or, better yet, just call her by her name! It works every time.

Understanding Her Perspective: What a Good Boss Needs to Know

1. She dislikes being called "sweetheart," "young lady," or any other diminishing term at work.
2. She doesn't want you to call her by a nickname that she didn't invite you to use.
3. It's difficult to correct people more than once when they continue to use the wrong name.
4. Not getting her name right makes her feel unimportant and marginalized.

Intermediate Level: Use the Correct Name—and Spell It and Say It Correctly

Casie, not Cassie. Stacey with an "ey" at the end. Kirsten, not Kristen. Krystal with a "K." These are all examples of women within my own company who experience the misspelling or mispronouncing of their names on a nearly daily basis. Once you start paying attention, you'll find these small indignities everywhere. Even if you're just getting a single letter wrong, when it comes to her name and her identity, every letter matters. I often have to correct people who write my assistant Gabi's name as "Gabby." It drives me crazy, and it drives her crazy too.

"It can be upsetting when my name is right there—usually in emails," Gabi said. "But it's most hurtful when it's someone I know well who misspelled it—such as a long-term colleague. It shows a carelessness and a lack of respect toward my individuality. Once on Slack, a colleague named Owen misspelled my name (and my user-name was Gabi, right there in front of him!). For the remainder of the day, I spelled his name 'Owin' on all general and group channels. He now spells my name correctly."

Shanelle, an HR executive, relayed her ongoing experience of being called the wrong name. "On the name front, I have been called Shantel, Shanellie, Cheryl, Sherell, and Shaneil. I politely correct them by restating my name every time it is said incorrectly. In email, the iPhone autocorrects my name to 'Shameless.' You would be amazed at how many emails I have gotten that start with 'Hi Shameless.'"*

It's even more of an issue for those with names from other ethnicities and cultures. People will ask them if there's another name they can call them or suggest that they should consider an Americanized version of their name. Or they will just repeatedly get it wrong. These repeated slights can add up to a message that "you don't belong here." Yasmin, a lawyer whose name is of Spanish origin, finds that people often call her "Jasmine" instead, and don't even seem to register that those are different names. "When I have corrected someone, they often continue to say it wrong," she shares.

---

* Autocorrect changes my name, Kate, to "Late." After hearing Shanelle's story, I thought maybe autocorrect is gender biased and converts female names to adjectives with negative connotations! I found no research evidence to support my theory, but for what it's worth, I think someone should look into this.

What's in a name?
A lot, especially if it's John.

The S&P 1500 has fewer female CEOs than CEOs named John.

The Democratic Party has fewer female governors than governors named John.

The Republican Party has fewer female senators than senators named John.

Johns represent 3.3 percent of the male population. Women represent 50.8 percent of the total population.[4]

I used to be reluctant to speak up when someone got my name wrong. I made up my own rule that if someone called me by the wrong name, I would correct them once. After that, I gave up; if they kept doing it, I would just let them call me the wrong name.

Lots of women take that approach, but just because they are quiet about it or say they don't mind doesn't mean it isn't having a negative impact. With those people who I decided not to keep correcting, I still heard it every time they said my name incorrectly. Even if only for a second, it distracted me from my work every time it happened. It disengaged me. It's harder to listen to someone who didn't listen to you when you told them your name.

Research on how men address women extends beyond the world of business to academic professions. A 2017 study found that men are more likely to address or introduce other men in the field of academic medicine by their title of *Doctor*, whereas men are more likely to address or introduce female doctors by their first name.[5] This extends to other fields as well. In politics, women are more likely to be addressed by their first names rather than their titles. In college, students are more likely to call a woman instructor by her first name than to address her as *Professor*.[6] Doing so minimizes the perceived expertise and authority of women.

Getting names right is also a big topic in school. Numerous studies in K–12 education highlight the importance of getting students' names right. Many label it a microaggression, often with racial or cultural undertones, when teachers don't respect and remember names.[7] The aftereffects can be long-lasting; if a child feels it's not worth a teacher's time to get their name right, school becomes a place where they feel less welcome and may question whether they can be successful.

Mollie Robertson, a high school math teacher in Kentucky, states it perfectly: "To fully accept and respect a student, you must at a minimum know how to pronounce their name."[8] If every manager followed that same simple rule for employees, we would have a more welcoming workplace for women. Getting all names right is undeniably important, but misnaming, nicknaming, and using unwanted terms of endearment are all things that happen more to women and to other underrepresented groups.

As a manager, recognize that names are important and prioritize getting them right. Don't excuse others, either. Consider yourself to be an active defender of proper name use in all business settings. Now, whenever I hear someone use the wrong name for a colleague, or mispronounce a name, I always correct it. I do not shy away from correcting people more than once, with some gentle teasing added for repeat offenders. I also double-check every email I write to make sure I've spelled all names correctly before I click *send*.

"Getting a name wrong is the absolute worst thing you can do as a salesperson," says Brian, a leader of a national sales team. "You can easily lose a sale over that. Clients need to feel that they are important to you, and how can they feel that way if you didn't even bother to learn their name? As a manager, it's just common sense to treat your employees' names with the same importance."

It's not hard to remember the name of someone who you work with, but it does take effort. You have to listen, remember, and sometimes do a little work to find a context clue if you forget. Ask if you are uncertain. If you know someone as Jennifer but hear someone else address her as Jenny, it's totally fine to ask, "Do you go by Jenny or do you prefer Jennifer?" If you are unsure about how to pronounce an unfamiliar name, it's also OK to ask. "I deal with an international audience and there are some very different vocalization patterns globally," shares Laurence, a lawyer. "So I've learned to say, 'Does it rhyme with . . . ?' as a way of testing my pronunciation to make sure I got it right."

In addition to names, pronoun use is important to get right as well. For anyone on your team who does not identify as gender binary (she/her/hers or he/him/his), make sure you know which pronouns they use. Just as calling someone by the wrong name is disrespectful, misgendering someone is equally problematic. Asking about preferences shows that you care about getting it right.

Finally, "I'm not good with names" is not a valid excuse. If you can't learn someone's name it means you are either not putting in the effort, or you have a weak ability to retain important information. Neither one of those things is something you want to be, especially in a work context. Anyone who can pay attention and retain information can be good with names. (See the CEO Perspective section at the end of this chapter for more pointers.)

Advanced Level: No Proactive Nicknames

Jessica Valenti at the *Guardian* wrote a column in 2014 expressing her frustration when colleagues addressed her as "Jessie," a nickname she had never actually used to introduce herself. [9] It's frustrating on a few different levels when this happens. Sometimes you're just getting their name wrong, which shows a lack of respect (see the previous section). Other times, it is intrusive; it suggests a familiarity that she didn't invite. In the most frustrating cases, it's condescending, diminishing a woman by using a younger, more girlish-sounding version of her actual name.

"I'd prefer a curse to a cutesy nickname," Valenti wrote. "Like most things men call women when they want to diminish them, 'Jessie' is meant to remind me that no matter what I accomplish—the number of books written, articles published, speeches given—I'm still 'just a girl.'"

The response to Valenti's column was viral and vocal; this is something so many women experience professionally. Women can readily pull examples of the nicknames men give them at work. Some women anecdotally cite that it seems to happen most during interactions where they are challenging a man on an issue of substance. He calls her by the nickname as a way of devaluing her.

Coverage of women in the press reinforces the existence of this behavior. Just look at how Hillary Clinton became "Hill" or Elizabeth Warren became "Lizzy" when their male adversaries were trying to bring them down in political interactions.

Correcting behavior in others is as important as regulating your own behavior when it comes to naming. When just asking someone to get it right doesn't work, I'll often try the tactic of nicknaming back: Mike gets called Mikey, Joe becomes Joey, and so on. My hope in calling them something they didn't asked to be called is that they will improve their awareness of the impact it has on others to misstate their names. People usually get the point.

If you're struggling with the formality of a no-nickname policy, or feeling self-conscious about not nicknaming women while you have an established pattern of nicknaming the men on your team, you might try the tactic of calling her by her last name. Last names are one notable exception to the rules of nicknames. Being referred to only by your surname is widely viewed as a mark of respect and a signal of power. And it's something that men do with each other, often at the exclusion of women. If this is something you do, consider including women. Basically, if you're feeling like you absolutely must call her by something other than her first name, try her last name!

Saving the Best for Last

Men are greater than 50 percent more likely to be called by their surnames at work.[10]

Students were 56 percent more likely to refer to a male professor by only his surname on Rate My Professors.[11]

Political pundits were 126 percent as likely to refer to men by their last names only on radio shows.[12]

Scientists identified by only their last names were considered 14 percent more worthy of receiving a National Science Foundation award.[13]

Expert Level: Get Her Last Name Right Even When It Changes

I got married in December, and one day after returning from our honeymoon, we attended Kaplan's annual holiday party, which our CEO, Jonathan, hosted at his house in Westchester. It was a big event. The top fifty or so executives of the company were invited, along with spouses and partners, and people traveled in from all our main offices, including Fort Lauderdale, Chicago, and London. It was the first time that I had been invited, having just that year risen to the level that made the cut.

Jonathan took me aside early in the evening and said he was planning to toast my recent marriage, and he wanted to know if I was changing my last name. I told him that, yes, I had decided to legally take my husband's last name. He then asked, "But what do you want to be called at work?" Until that moment I hadn't really thought about the impact that a name change would have on my professional identity. I froze.

He said, "OK, you need to think about it, and I'll come back and ask you again." Typical to his style, he only gave me about ten minutes. But ten minutes was enough time to know what I wanted. My instinct was telling me that I wasn't ready to let go of my maiden name. I felt that changing the name I had used professionally for so many years would amount to abandoning the reputation I had built under it. But I had always planned to take Chris's last name when we married, and it was important to me to have the same last name as the children we hoped to have. I had seen women use different names for different contexts; her husband's last name for personal things, and her maiden name for a professional identity. But my personal identity was pretty wrapped up in my professional one, so I wasn't so sure about that.

Under the pressure of ten minutes came clarity: I decided to use both names all the time. Thus, in a flash, I made what I've come to realize was an important decision for own my identity and my name: I would be Kate Eberle Walker. When Jonathan gathered everyone together, he made a toast, and asked everyone to raise a glass to "the newlyweds, Kate Eberle Walker and her husband, Chris Walker." And that was that; I was Kate Eberle Walker.

Or so I thought. In the weeks, months, and years that followed, very few people actually called me Kate Eberle Walker. They all had their reasons why they chose not to call me what I had asked to be called.

"Kate Eberle Walker? That's a mouthful. It's too long."

"I'm just going to call you Kate Walker. It's easier to remember."

"I've known you as Kate Eberle for so long. I can't change it now."

"What does your husband think about your name? Isn't it kind of only going halfway into a marriage?"

"Did you know that when women don't take their husband's last name they are statistically more likely to get divorced?"*

When women get married, they grapple with this major decision around a name change, reconciling how they feel about it professionally and personally. It's a big deal and a lot of thought goes into it. Approximately 30 percent of women either keep their maiden name entirely or continue to use it in a professional context.[14] This can be a loaded decision; a 2010 study found that women who do not take their husband's name professionally are perceived to be "more independent, more ambitious, more intelligent, and more competent." That's great. But . . . they are also viewed as "less caring."[15] Ouch. That's a pretty rough judgment to bring down on someone because she felt an unbreakable connection to the name she grew up with.

For many years after I got married, I let people call me whatever *they* wanted instead of speaking up about what *I* wanted. I became self-conscious about the length and complexity of my name. I was doing M&A work then, so most of the time the people that I was interacting with were investment bankers, lawyers, business owners,

---

* Let's talk about this one. That "fact" was told to me with such authority that I took it at face value and believed it for more than twelve years. But it appears to be a myth. I dug around for research that demonstrated a statistically higher instance of divorce among heterosexual couples where the wife did not take the husband's last name, and I could not find any such research.

and private equity investors. Mostly men, and mostly older than me. Sometimes I would make a phone call and say, "Hi, it's Kate Eberle Walker," and the person on the other end, especially if it was a much older man, would reply, "What? Sorry, I didn't catch that." So I started just saying, "Hi, it's Kate from Kaplan," when I called.

I had chosen to keep my maiden name because it mattered to my identity. Yet despite making that choice, I was inconsistent in enforcing it. I discovered that if I didn't make a strong push to change what people called me, they would make the decision for me. So I let people call me Kate Eberle or Kate Walker, not liking it but not wanting to make it a big deal.

It wasn't until I became a CEO that I had the confidence to insist that people call me by both last names, Kate Eberle Walker. And that's when I realized how much it matters. I felt so much more comfortable and accepted in a work environment where people call me what I asked to be called. I've become unapologetic about it, but still find that I have to repeat it again and again to prevent the slide of others into their own comfort zones of what they'd like to call me.

As a manager you should know that when a woman on your team changes her name, or doesn't, she thought about those decisions much more deeply than you or anyone else did. She has good reasons for the choices she made. Give her the respect of calling her what she asks you to call her. Without comment, and with effort. Sure, it's hard to get used to calling someone by a different name, especially if you worked together for years before she changed it. Mistakes and slipups are normal. But try. Try to get it right, apologize when you get it wrong, and acknowledge that it's your responsibility to learn it. Introduce her to others correctly, using the complete name she has chosen, and when people get it wrong, correct them. Doing all of this will reduce friction and frustration in her everyday work experience and will help her to feel respected and comfortable in her own identity at work.

Good Boss Checklist: What You Can Do to Be a Better Boss for Women

1. Don't call her *sweetheart*. Or *sweetie, sugar, honey, dear,* or *young lady.*
2. Don't use a nickname if she introduced herself by her full name.
3. Call her by her correct name. Spell it correctly. Pronounce it correctly.
4. If she changes her name, use the new name she gives you.
5. Correct others who get her name wrong.

THE CEO PERSPECTIVE:
BIG IDEAS FOR COMPANY-WIDE IMPACT

Leading Hotels of the World:
A System for Learning Names

Leading Hotels of the World (LHW) has 265 employees worldwide,* with the majority in sales and marketing roles, interacting with hotel owners, managers, and travel agencies all over the world. In hospitality, remembering names takes on outsized importance. To give a hotel guest the feeling that they are truly a valued customer receiving special, personalized treatment, it's of paramount importance to the five-star hotel experience to call guests by their names. This philosophy carries over into the ethos of LHW as a core value.

People in the hospitality business also know that it's not easy to learn names, remember them, and pronounce them properly, especially when interacting across multiple languages and cultures. So they use strategies and processes to improve their ability to successfully call people by their names.

"It's deceptively simple to say, 'We work hard to get every name right,'" says LHW CEO Shannon Knapp. "It's not just something you say you're going to do—you have to approach it with a process. The first thing that I tell people is, you have to pay attention so that you actually hear the name when it is told to you. Active listening is at least half of getting it right. When I'm meeting someone for the first time, I have learned to consciously pause, stop thinking

---

* Full disclosure: my husband is one of those employees!

about whatever else was going on in my mind, and focus on hearing the name when it is told to me."

Even with active focus, you're not going to reach 100 percent success in remembering every name that you hear. The next step is more active listening.

"If you've forgotten a name that you think you should know, you need to listen to the context clues available to you," Knapp advises. As you are talking, look for memory joggers that will take you back to that first conversation when you learned the person's name. Often something will trigger the memory and it will come back to you. Or, you might get lucky and receive the ultimate context clue—someone else greeting the person by name as you are talking.

The final step is to line up help by using other tools and supports available to you. "The world's best creation are name badges at conferences and business cards," says Knapp. The key is to use them. Another important component is establishing a process for having others ask the question so that you don't have to ask again. At LHW, colleagues know that if they join a conversation and their colleague doesn't introduce them, that's their cue to introduce themselves and get the other person to restate their name.

Throughout the process, LHW has found that the key to success is really about giving every individual the respect of listening to them with focus and attention. "It's the same philosophy that I instill in all of our leaders," Knapp concludes. "The trick is always to actually be listening."

The Big Idea

Create a business process for getting names right.

Why It Works

- Treats getting the name right as a must-do, not a nice-to-do.
- Success comes from active listening.
- Conveys respect to every individual by taking on the work involved in getting a name right, rather than expecting the individual to do the work of repeating herself.

RULE #2

BE SOMEONE SHE CAN RELATE TO

An employee needs to be able to trust their manager. Trust that you have their best interests at heart, trust that you will have their back, and trust that you will give them credit for the work that they do. A big part of that comes from just believing that your manager is a decent person, and even better, someone who you like. Think of the bosses you've had in your career. A subset of them are probably still your friends today. And it's likely that it's those people that you did your best work for, and who did the most for you. The key to being a good manager for anyone, not just for women, is to establish a friendship with them.

There are two motivators that generally get the best work out of someone: fear or trust. People do good work for you because they like you and they believe you have their best interests at heart, or because they are scared of the consequences of not doing what you asked. One of these works way better than the other. (If you want to stick with fear, you may want to skip ahead to Rule #8: Be an Equal Opportunity Asshole. Otherwise, let's continue.) The key to the "trusted manager" approach is to connect with your team not just through the work but through a shared appreciation for other priorities in your lives.

Embrace Your Similarities

When I tell male managers that they need to be relatable to their female employees, the most common response that I get is, "But I can't be a woman, so what am I supposed to do?" To be honest, I find this abdication of responsibility really annoying. Literally no one has ever told me it's OK not to try to relate to my male employees, or my employees of color, or my LGBTQ employees, because I am a straight white woman. While it might be easiest to relate to someone who has an obvious thing in common with you, like gender, race or sexual preference, that's not the only way. As a manager, you don't need to have *everything* in common with an employee to relate to her; you just need to have *something* that connects you. Whether you went to the same college, have a similar hobby, or a shared passion for your company's mission, reinforce the commonalities.

I once had a boss who was exactly as obsessed with New York real estate as I was. We used to talk about apartment listings over lunch and I still send him listings every now and then. Another time, I was the boss and discovered that a guy who worked for me was just as dedicated to his gym workouts as I was. It doesn't have to be anything extraordinary, just something you both like to talk about.

Another woman reflected on her friendship with a boss who worked remotely. They discovered that they both really liked to play tennis. She only saw him about ten days out of the year, but whenever they did get together, they made a point of playing tennis. It doesn't really matter what it is—the point is just to find something you both like, and connect through it.

Be Authentic

Ann, an executive, shared a story of a first-time manager who came to her for advice about how to interact with a woman on his team. "He told me he thought he made a mistake. He said to me, 'I admitted I stayed home to work for the day because I didn't want to get stuck in traffic on my way home from the office and miss *The Bachelor* on TV tonight.'*

---

* If you really want a foolproof way to connect with more women on your team, watch *The Bachelor* and be prepared to join in the postgame analysis the following morning. I'm not ashamed to admit that I've lost countless hours to analyzing this show with the women on my teams. It's a universal connector.

"I told him, I thought that was probably the best thing he'd done all day. He's a disciplined, serious person at work, and saying that gave insight into his less disciplined side. He was a person who would adjust his work schedule to be sure he got to watch a favorite TV show. When you talk about the things you care about, it gives you another dimension besides being just a twenty-four-year-old who comes in and works hard. Maybe now she sees you as someone to whom she can say, 'I know this may seem stupid to you, but can I leave early today because . . .'

"Being your authentic self is so important. If there's not more to your life than work, you're not going to be a good manager. If you can't share about yourself outside of work, you're not going to be a good manager."

Be Fallible

Carly, a finance professional, recalled a time that one of her direct reports made a mistake that many of us have made in our careers: the dreaded *reply all* when you meant to reply directly to a single individual on an email. Carly had sent her analyst a work request and copied the client and the senior team members. The analyst had meant to reply only to Carly, saying, "I don't understand why they're asking for this," but accidentally clicked *reply all* and included everyone else, including the client, on the message.

It was a screwup, for sure. But Carly took the opportunity to share a story about herself that was equally cringeworthy. When Carly, an Ohio University alumnus, was a new analyst at Goldman Sachs, she sent an email to a very senior partner, a fellow OU alum, asking him to complete a survey she had created for alumni to share insights from their career paths to help future OU grads.

"When I first got to GS, I sent him an email introducing myself and attaching the survey. There was this rule at GS that every email had to be answered, no matter how senior the recipient or how junior the sender. But still, my message wasn't exactly work-related, and I was brand new, so I didn't know if he would reply. Nonetheless I was envisioning an enthusiastic welcome to Goldman, or at least a 'happy to help.' He did reply. He said 'OK.' That's it. I forwarded the email to my boyfriend (or I meant to . . .) and I wrote, 'Hope his survey answers are more verbose than this. Love you love you love you.' But I didn't click *forward*—I clicked *reply*. I sent that email to the senior partner!"

Carly's openness about her own blunder made her direct report feel better and illustrated that everyone makes mistakes and goes on to live another day. It also generated trust between them because Carly had been willing to open up and reveal that she was not perfect. It made her more accessible. For a manager, there's almost nothing more valuable than having your employees feel comfortable admitting their mistakes to you. It's so much easier to fix something if you know about it proactively instead of finding out about it reactively. You want people to come to you when they think they've done something wrong, and not just because they trust that you won't blow up at them, but because they believe that you can actually help them resolve a bad situation and make it better.

There's nothing more relatable than humility. No one is perfect and your direct reports will like you better if you are open with them about the mistakes you've made in your own career. Share your story of your own path to promotion. How did you get your job? Where was luck involved versus hard work? What do you wish you'd done differently?

Just one note of caution: being honest about your past mistakes is different from being open about your current insecurities. Most employees want confident managers, and they want to feel like they are working for someone who they can learn from and who knows what they're doing. You can be more honest than you were in the job interview when someone asked you to describe your three greatest weaknesses, but don't fully unload on your direct reports about what keeps you up at night either.

Be Genuinely Interested in People

Everyone loved my boss Gerry. We used to travel all around the world working on deals, and no matter where we went, Gerry was a favorite. He was a brilliant man, possibly the smartest person I've ever worked for. But that's not why everyone loved him. He was tremendously curious and interested in getting to know everyone he met. He didn't need to find a particular hobby or shared interest to connect with people. Everyone likes talking about themselves, and everyone likes when people think they are worth listening to. So it's brilliantly simple: connect with people simply by caring about who they are and taking the time to learn about their lives.

One time we were in Brazil visiting a company that we were exploring a deal with. Gerry asked the owner of the company to tell us about the history of the company.* He sat captivated as the owner

---

* Funny side note: The owner had a distinctive Brazilian accent, which I wasn't yet conversant in. He told us about his family company's origins as a maker of "magical equipment." They had become the first and largest maker of magical equipment in Brazil, and as competition entered the space, his grandfather had the foresight to realize the market was shifting and to move the company away from making magical equipment to building and running a school. It was that school that Gerry and I had come to Brazil to explore a deal with. No wonder Gerry was captivated by the conversation, I thought. What an incredible pivot from making magic wands to running a medical school entrance exam test preparation service! Turns out, the owner was saying *medical equipment*. That made more sense.

told the story, peppering his reactions with exclamations. "Well, isn't that wonderful!" "Incredible!" We listened to the family history for at least thirty minutes before we ever got to asking anything about the business we were there to see. This was a company that many other competitors were also interested in buying, but they wanted to sell to us because they trusted Gerry.

His approach translated to his management of me as well. He knew all about me: who I was, why I worked, and what I did best. When we traveled, he knew what kind of food I liked to eat. We would go to the most interesting places when we dined out, not because he wanted to eat there, but because he wanted me to experience it. I think of it now as "selfless management." I felt so good about the work I was doing when I worked for him, and when you feel good about your work you make it better. It has been more than fifteen years since I worked for him, but to this day, whenever I reach out to him, he makes me feel important and interesting in every conversation we have.

Understanding Her Perspective: What a Good Boss Needs to Know

1. If she trusts you and believes that you have her back, she will return the loyalty.
2. She will find it easier to connect with you if you open up about your own life and priorities.
3. She has historically been given female mentors, but there's no reason she can't have male mentors too.
4. She values authenticity.

Talk About Your Family

Often an easy thing to connect on is your family life. Talking about your family and the time you spend with them outside of the office can show her a path that resonates, a way to be successful at work while also prioritizing home life. Plus, people just like talking about their kids.

Sam, a CEO, believes, "The fact that I have a working wife and three kids changes the dynamic between me and my direct reports. Three out of five on my exec team are women. Being able to relate to them, to say, 'My wife is speaking at a conference in Switzerland this week, so I've got the kids for the next three days,' matters. They know I'm in it, experiencing the same things that they are. So they can be more comfortable talking about their own things."

Susan, a sales manager, recalls that her boss used to schedule their one-on-one check-in calls to coincide with his commute so that he could make the most of his driving time. He would sometimes end their calls very abruptly when he pulled into his driveway if he saw his kids waiting there. "He would say, 'I gotta go. I don't want my kids to have to wait while I finish a call; I don't want them to ever think they're not the most important thing,'" Susan reflected. "At the time I didn't even have kids of my own, but I appreciated his openness about who he was and what he cared about."

One year my company holiday party was scheduled on the same date and time as my daughters' school holiday concert. The schedule had been out of my control because we were one portfolio company of many, attending a joint party hosted by our owners. I was the CEO, so it would certainly be noticed if I didn't show up at the holiday party. But my daughters' concert was a major event. Every parent attended, and it mattered deeply to my girls that I be there. Perhaps if I'd been traveling they might have been able to understand, but to be in the city, and to choose to go to a party instead of coming to see them play their instruments, sing their songs, and celebrate the beginning of the holiday break would be devastating. So it wasn't even a tough decision. I would be skipping my company party and going to the girls' concert.

I did need to let my employees know that I wasn't going to be there, and I needed to explain why. I sent an email to everyone in the company, explaining the situation and how important it was to my kids and to me that I be there for the concert. I wished them a happy party and said I couldn't wait to hear about it the next day. I thought that my teams would understand, and maybe even have more fun at a party where the CEO wasn't watching! What I didn't expect was the outpouring of responses that I received from other working moms.

"I've never had a CEO who was so honest about balancing work and kids."

"You just made me feel one hundred times better about times when I miss out on a work event to spend time with my family."

"I feel like you really understand the trade-offs working parents make."

People appreciate knowing that their managers grapple with the same things that they do. We all have competing obligations and we experience stress over the choices we make. Sharing that you face those dilemmas, too, and showing that sometimes you choose family over work, makes you more real to the people you manage.

It's OK to Mix the Personal and the Professional (Just Don't Make It Weird)

It's more fun to work in a place where people really know each other. When you make it comfortable for your team to talk about how they spend their time outside work, there is more trust and empathy among coworkers. You can't be as effective as a manager if you don't really understand how your employees are spending their time, and your employee can't be fully happy at work if she's hiding parts of her day-to-day reality.

There's a lot that we are told not to ask when it comes to inter-actions with employees. Don't pry about their home lives, don't ask about their dating lives, don't be nosy. I've always struggled with this dilemma: You're not supposed to ask people about who they really are outside of work, but how can you really know them if you don't? I once sent out an internal email celebrating the fact that our executive team was 20 percent LGBTQ and sharing why I thought it was important to be representative not just of gender but of other underrepresented groups as well. Sending that message telegraphed to our LGBTQ employees that I was supportive of them and that I cared about representing them. I started getting emails and having conversations with people who wanted to tell me about themselves, about their families, their same-sex significant others, and the lives they had. They told me a lot of things that I never would have asked but I was so glad to know. Sometimes the right thing to do is not to ask, but to make it evident that you want to know, if they want to tell you.

Connect Positive Feedback to Leadership Qualities

Part of your job as a manager is to identify the skills, talent, and potential in your direct reports. When you give positive feedback about something, try to connect it to a similar skill seen in one of the senior executives of the company. Point out to your own team, "Your problem-solving approach is very similar to David's." Or "Your pre-sentation style really reminds me of Joe's." The goal is to help your direct reports look up in the organization and see themselves in the leaders so that they can think to themselves, "I can do that too."

Why Representative Role Models Matter

It's very hard for anyone to picture themselves being successful at something when they've never seen anyone like them do it before. This is a big part of why anyone in a minority position, whether due to gender, race, or lifestyle, often struggles to see themselves in positions of power. If you're not a white male, you have to have a lot more imagination when envisioning your future as a powerful executive. Whereas when you have something in common with someone and then watch them succeed, you think, "That could be me."

Diversifying CEOs and executive teams is not the only way to provide relatable role models, but it's the best way. For example, working environments that are not designed by people of color, with people of color in mind, will not be as conducive to their success. Leaders need to change the dynamic, and to do that we need more diverse representation in leadership positions. The more role models your company represents, whether by gender, race, ethnicity, or sexual orientation, the better the chance that the young talent on your teams will be able to look up and see someone that reminds them of themselves. And when they see that, they will much more readily picture themselves doing that job in the future.

Of course, it's not possible for every company to represent every attribute of every employee in its management ranks. When I once proudly highlighted in a company meeting that 50 percent of our executive team was female, I received many appreciative emails from female employees. They shared that for the first time they felt truly seen and represented at work, and it made them more committed to the company to feel like we valued people like them at our most senior levels. But I also got an email from a sales manager in our organization whose ethnicity was Hispanic. He wrote, "I look at our leadership team and I don't see anyone who looks like me. I can't help but wonder 'What about me?'"

It was a fair question, and it helped me evolve my definition of "success" in terms of diverse representation. When you emphasize representation for any single group, women included, you are de-emphasizing others. This doesn't mean that you shouldn't celebrate improvements in representation. But you should celebrate them as progress, not ultimate success. I now think about diversity goals as progressive steps.

A good first step toward diversity is to eliminate any single standard or majority on a team—taking proactive action to address structures where the majority of the management team are men, or the majority of the board of directors are white, for example. Reducing majorities helps all of those who are not yet represented at least feel that the possibility of them becoming leaders is more realistic: there isn't one type that they are not; there are many models of success. Why not them too?

Another step toward diversity is to set a goal to not have only one of any group on a team. Being the only one feels isolating and uncomfortable. You're always conscious of being different and thinking about ways to blend in. An employee once shared with me that she was often in work situations where she was the only one: the only woman, the only Black person, the only gay person. She said, "My teammates are naturally more relaxed than I am because they are surrounded by comfortable sameness. I wonder how much more successful I'd be if I wasn't always battling this self-consciousness of being different." There is tremendous comfort in not being alone. Having one woman on a team is good, but having two women is much more impactful. Having two Black people on a team is exponentially better than one. And so on. Again, you can't represent every single type of person on every single team, but that shouldn't stop you from doing as much as possible. Diverse representation doesn't just matter for the individuals on your team—it also matters for the company's bottom line. See The CEO Perspective: Rosetta Stone: Board Representation on page 134.

Embrace Social Media

Many people live their lives on social media, or at least give you a very open window into their lives. And they are happy for you to participate, maybe even appreciative of the extra likes and follows. In today's era of social media, I follow clear rules for engagement with my professional contacts, colleagues, and employees. I directly communicate to employees what my rules of engagement are for personal sharing.

I ask all employees to connect with me on LinkedIn so that we can collectively make the most of our networks on behalf of the company. I want a salesperson, for example, to be able to see who I know so that he can ask for introductions when helpful. Twitter is where I share thoughts and interesting information relevant for our company and our market. I encourage people to follow and interact with me there, but no obligation. Finally, I tell them that my Instagram is for personal sharing, where I talk about my home, the plays I see, and the books I read, and, mostly, I share lots and lots of posts about my kids. I tell my colleagues that they are welcome to follow my account if they're interested in knowing me. I won't proactively follow them, but if they reach out and tell me it's OK, then I will, because I like to know everything that people are willing to share with me about themselves. Not everyone takes me up on that,* but many people do, and I love getting to see them hanging out with friends and families, going on vacations, walking their dogs, and planting things in their backyards.

Many managers don't engage in social media interactions with employees, or still ascribe to outdated policies like "It's never appropriate to connect with coworkers online," or "My Facebook should only be for my immediate family." I often tell people on my executive team things about their own direct reports that they don't know but lots of other people in the company do, because we're all connected

---

* To be fair, some people not only don't take me up on it, but they post on Glassdoor that I only took my CEO job "so I could get more Instagram followers." So, opening up your social media is not necessarily a universally popular move. I do, however, believe there are proven, easier ways to get Instagram followers than taking a job as a CEO, so I wouldn't recommend doing it for that purpose.

on social media. To me, connecting with people in this way is one of the easiest ways to build genuine rapport. It's fun, it's easy, and it's curated; they control what they post and share, and so do you. Especially as remote working becomes more prevalent, social media sharing can replace some of what's lost from not having social time together at an office.

The COVID-19 pandemic, and the era of widespread working from home that it introduced, launched the workplace into a new era of intimacy. People got to peek at each other's artwork, meet their pets, and in many cases watch kids move on- and off-screen. We all got to know each other better, and in the process, work became more personal. The broader shift to working from home started far earlier as technology developments and internet connectivity allowed for more jobs to be done remotely, and it has steadily introduced more elements of home life into the workday. This increased blending of home and work makes it easier to get to know who people really are. It's no longer even possible to tune out the personal elements of a coworker's life, so I say, embrace it.

Remember, She's Not Your Wife, Mom, or Daughter . . . and Definitely Not Your Girlfriend

Professional relationships are human relationships, and it's normal to try to reference relationships you've had with others to help you better understand the person sitting in front of you in your office. But you must always keep context in mind. The dynamics of a personal relationship you've had with a woman (your mom, your daughter, your girlfriend, your wife) do not translate to the dynamics you should expect in a professional relationship with a woman.

My last words of wisdom in this section are . . . in an effort to relate to the women on your team, please don't do so as you would in the personal realm. It's a natural tendency to make assumptions about priorities and motivations of others based on your own household.

When I interview for jobs that require a lot of travel and/or a major time commitment, and the interviewer learns that I am married with two young children, I find that many men who interview me get hung up on thinking about how this would work in their house. Would his wife be able to manage such a demanding job? If she had such a job, what would it mean for him? They struggle to separate their own household situation from mine, and sometimes switch from asking about me to asking about what my husband does, does he travel, how do I handle it all, and so on. Needless to say, this is totally inappropriate interview fodder. What it would mean for him if his wife had the job really has nothing to do with whether or not I can handle the job.

We all struggle to apply human lessons to people when we meet them. And, for most men, their reference point for a woman they know and understand well is not another female colleague; it's their wife. Women often report better working relationships with men who have wives working in comparable jobs outside the home. These men can better understand how families balance a dual-job household. But is that really the solution? It might be a while before every man is married to an analogous woman, especially considering that some marry men and others never marry.

Good Boss Checklist: What You Can Do to Be a Better Boss for Women

1. Be authentic. The best way to be relatable is to be open about who you are.
2. Connect. Highlight what you have in common beyond gender.
3. Listen. Pay attention to who your team members are and show them you care about knowing them.
4. Share. On social media or in conversations.
5. Confess. Talk about your flaws and mistakes, not just your successes.

THE CEO PERSPECTIVE: BIG IDEAS FOR COMPANY-WIDE IMPACT

Techstars: Using Personality Testing to Define Identity Outside of Gender

At Techstars, every employee takes a personality test called the DiSC as part of their orientation process. Based in Boulder, Colorado, Techstars has more than three hundred employees, and every one of them knows their DiSC profile. The DiSC is self-described as follows:

> [A] nonjudgmental tool used for discussion of people's behavioral differences . . . The DiSC model provides a common language that people can use to better understand themselves and to adapt their behaviors with others—within a work team, a sales relationship, a leadership position, or other relationships.[1]

The assessment starts managers and their employees off with a more nuanced understanding of each other's work styles and communication needs, which goes a long way toward helping them to establish positive working relationships. And because it is used throughout the organization, it also offers a common language that can help everyone understand the working style of their colleagues.

"People openly share their DiSC profiles, and it helps in knowing how to interpret what individuals say and how they might be interpreting what you're saying," shares David Brown, founder and CEO of Techstars. "It's not uncommon to hear 'I'm a D, but he's an I' types of statements as people debrief on work interactions."

The DiSC process was put into place at Techstars as part of early efforts to add data to otherwise subjective interactions. But having that shorthand identifier has also proven to be helpful in reducing focus on gender differences, Brown believes. "Knowing that someone is a D versus an I is a better label than identifying them as a man versus a woman. It reduces bias in other areas by shifting the differentiators to attributes that are shared across genders."

The proof is in the numbers. Techstars is among the rare group of companies where the gender balance of its executive team matches the gender split of its overall employee base, at fifty-fifty in both cases. This means that the Techstars management approach is not only attracting and hiring female talent, but it is also supporting and developing that talent to its top executive levels.

The Big Idea

Use a personality test for all employees.

Why It Works

- Shifts identity focus away from gender to other defining characteristics.
- Creates points of relatability that cross gender lines.
- Helps managers adapt their communication style to each employee's needs to create more positive working relationships.

RULE #3

DON'T ASK, "WHAT DOES YOUR HUSBAND DO?"

Selena Coppock is the comedian behind the popular Instagram account @NYTVows, which parodies the *New York Times* wedding pages, shining a light on the cultural trends underlying the nuptials of the privileged set. Selena has been reading the wedding pages since she was twelve years old. In the early days of building her following, which was originally on Twitter, some of her most popular tweets touched on the subject of women who stop working once they get married:

> "Until last week, the bride worked."
> "The bride earned a bachelor's degree in Russian Studies from Yale & master's degree in social work from NYU, neither of which she uses."[1]

A typical *New York Times* wedding page entry lists the couple's names, includes a polished photograph of the smiling couple and several paragraphs detailing the story of how they met, along with their education, careers, and family backgrounds. Many of the women on these pages have Ivy League degrees, work for blue-chip companies, and seem to have it all. But the phrase "until recently" was, and still is, frequently seen among the pages. As in, "The groom works at Merrill Lynch and the bride, until recently, worked at Goldman Sachs."

These women, it seemed, had not been working to pursue their own ambitions; they were just biding their time until they landed a husband, and then they stopped. The implication, that women only work if they have to, not because they want to, has become a lasting myth. The reasons behind these decisions, of course, are varied and complicated: perhaps they relocated geographically, perhaps they decided that if they wanted to have kids they couldn't sustain two high-pressure jobs between them, or perhaps she simply saw an opportunity to use the wedding as a natural breaking point to leave an imperfect job in pursuit of a better one.

"It has always been a thing," Coppock confirmed, "this sense that when women of privilege marry, they stop working. That women only want to work if they economically need to work. I'm surprised by how often it still comes up. My mom grew up in Manhattan on the Upper East Side, and that's how it really was for her generation. She was very discouraged from going to college. Women didn't go to college; it's just not what you do. It was seen as very déclassé to work."

My own mother, who met my father in the late 1960s when they were both working at the same bank, had a similar perspective. She was his career equal and, as she still likes to point out, a far better student. But once they got married, she stopped working. "That was just what you did back then," she explained to me. "Wives didn't work." Needless to say, this was not true for all women of that generation—we've heard the stories of the trailblazing women of my mother's generation who ran Fortune 500 companies, were appointed to the Supreme Court, and became secretary of state, to name a few. But this wasn't the norm. The norm was my mom's scenario: wives didn't work.

In 1950, fewer than 25 percent of married women worked, versus 70 percent of unmarried women. The gap was dramatic. But that gap continued to close as the percentage of married women in the workforce steadily increased. In today's world, whether or not a woman is married has very little to do with whether or not she works. Nearly 75 percent of married women work, compared to 80 percent of unmarried women.[2]

While much has changed across generations, a perception lingers that when a woman marries, her career becomes discretionary. Her income becomes a "second income." The implication is that women don't necessarily want to work, and so if they have a husband to support them, they won't. The mere appearance of an engagement ring can be interpreted as a signal that perhaps a woman will opt out of working life after the wedding.

The term "marriage penalty" is commonly used in the context of taxes. But there is also a marriage penalty that applies to the treatment of women in the workplace once they marry. Studies have estimated that women's earnings decline by 10 percent once married, whereas men enjoy a "marriage premium," earning as much as 40 percent more than their single male counterparts.[3]

When published in 2013, *Lean In* shared a statistic that caught the attention of many: 43 percent of married women with children leave the workforce. As a boss, it's hard to ignore that statistic, but it's also important to take it in the right context. It's not just after marriage when these 43 percent of wives leave the workforce; it's after having one or more children. When your employee comes in with a ring on her finger, you've still got a lot of time before she even actually gets married, let alone has kids. First, 20 percent of engagements are broken off and do not result in marriage.[4] For those that do proceed to marriage, on average, an engagement lasts 13.6 months, and couples in the United States wait three years after marriage before having their first child.[5] So we're talking about more than four years before kids are likely to even be a factor. By coincidence, guess what the median tenure is for an employee to stay at a company? It's 4.2 years.[6] So, by the time anyone gets around to having kids following an engagement, they probably will have changed jobs anyway.

And she may decide not to have kids at all. An increasing number of married couples are opting not to have children.* With so many different family structures, married couples with children are no longer the primary household structure. The percent of US

---

* According to Selena Coppock, there's a term for this. DINKS: Double Income, No Kids.

Who Knew?

Across the fifty states, residents of Utah wait the longest after marriage to start having children. Utahns (yes, that's the technical term) wait 4.7 years to have their first child.

Louisianans, on the other hand, are the quickest to get going after marriage. They wait only 1.9 years to have their first child.

households containing a married couple with children has fallen to only 19 percent.[7] So it's entirely possible that she will not have children either now or later.

Finally, remember that if a woman does marry and have children, that 43 percent statistic from *Lean In* has another side to it: 57 percent of married women with children do *not* leave the workplace. So, regardless of whether she has kids now, kids later, or kids never, the act of her getting married should not lead you to conclude that a woman is less committed to working. The statistics say that, more likely than not, she will continue working after getting married and after having children. That's all you need to know. Assume she wants to work, and that she will continue to work.

Some women have solved this issue by taking their rings off before they head into the office. But as we covered in Rule #2, the best working relationships come when people genuinely know each other and understand what's important to each other, inside and outside the workplace. So I don't like the idea of shying away from asking people about their relationships or families, or setting up a dynamic where she's better off hiding things about her life from you. Those things matter and are part of the identity of each of your team members. Don't make her hide her ring from you. Take responsibility as a boss to stop yourself from making judgments about career ambition based on seeing an engagement ring, hearing about wedding plans, or hearing about anything other than work that is important to her.

Understanding Her Perspective: What a Good Boss Needs to Know

1. She works because she wants to work.
2. She cares about being financially independent.
3. She wants to be paid what she's worth, not what you think she needs.
4. She's not necessarily planning to have children, and if she is, it may be a long way off.

Assumptions about marriage and work commitment can get in the way of being a good manager. Here are situations to pay extra attention to in checking your own assumptions.

Job Offers: Don't Consider Whether or Not a Candidate Is Married When Making a Job Offer

Anne, a technology executive with an MBA from Harvard, built many years of experience in high-paying jobs in finance. Over the course of those years, she also got married. She decided that she wanted to pursue an operating executive position at a startup, excited to find something that she would be passionate about. As she discussed potential opportunities with executive recruiters, she was surprised to discover that the same question kept coming up.

"Several recruiters I spoke to asked me, 'What does your husband do?'" she recalled. "I thought, *This is weird—why do they keep asking that?* In one of these conversations, I just got fed up, and I said, 'I don't see how that is relevant.'"

The recruiter defended her question. "She said, 'It's very relevant since you are interviewing with startups. It helps us understand your flexibility and ability to take risk in your compensation to know if your income is primary or secondary in your household.'"

"What my husband does has nothing to do with whether or not I'm qualified for the job," Anne recalled. "If they want to hire me, they should make me an offer. I'm perfectly capable of making my own assessment of what I need or want in my compensation."

The recruiter went on to insist that there really wasn't any gender bias underlying her question because she asked it in every single interview she conducted. "Really?" Anne asked with her eyebrows raised. "You ask every man you interview what his partner does?"

Here's the thing: even if the recruiter was asking that question of everyone, it's not a good question to ask *anyone*, regardless of gender. It's not an innocent question; it's loaded. In Anne's case, the question behind the question was, "What does your husband do that *allows you* to take on the risk of a startup salary?"

What someone's spouse makes, or whether the individual is independently wealthy, or whether someone has a spouse at all, for that matter, should have no bearing on whether or not you hire them and what you pay them for their work. I'm not sure which is worse: not hiring someone because you think she needs more money than what you can pay, or hiring her because you think you can get her for cheap since her husband makes a lot of money. Both are pretty terrible. When making job offers, stick to making hiring choices based on who is the best person for the job, and stick to making compensation offers based on what the role is worth.

Work Opportunities: Don't Make Assumptions About Whether or Not a Woman Wants to Travel, Take On More Responsibility, or Otherwise Continue Working Hard After She Gets Married

Shortly after I got married, I attended a company dinner where I found myself seated next to the president of one of our largest divisions.

"Congratulations on your wedding," he began our friendly conversation. He continued, "So you've been traveling a lot this past year . . ."

It was true, I had been traveling extensively, spending weeks at a time in Australia working on several acquisitions. I loved it there, enjoyed the team that I was working with, and was part of building an important new arm of the company. I was glad that the work was getting noticed by executives around the company. I started telling a story about the deal that we had recently closed in Sydney.

He interrupted, "Those are big trips; do you think you'll keep that up?"

Seeing the confused look on my face, he elaborated. "I mean, you must miss your husband when you're gone for so long."

Oh, I realized, *he meant, will I keep that up now that I'm married.* I felt my professional identity had shifted in a way I hadn't anticipated. I was no longer being evaluated solely as an independent individual; I was now thought of, at least partly, in relation to my husband. I worried that the perception of my potential and ambition was shrinking. There were deeper questions underlying the dinner chatter: Would I still work? Would I have kids, and when? Was I a good wife if I was always flying halfway around the world, leaving my husband behind in New York? Maybe he didn't mean to set off all those questions in my mind, but I heard judgment in his comments.

It can be very easy to slip into assumptions when observing and talking about the life changes of coworkers. Sometimes you don't even realize you're doing it. One morning I headed to an 8:30 AM finance committee meeting. As the group was convening and getting settled, we gathered around the conference table chatting as we waited to start the meeting. The conversation centered on the particularly large diamond on the newly acquired engagement ring of a junior accountant on the team. She had not yet entered the room.

"Did you see the size of that ring?" said one woman in a stage whisper.

"Her fiancé has a lot of money," another colleague chimed in.

A third added, "She has a really long commute—do you think she'll keep that up after the wedding?"

Just like that, the conversation had started with seemingly innocent gossip about an engagement but had quickly moved into the dangerous territory of making assumptions about whether or not she would keep working. The group was questioning the work commitment and ambition of someone who wasn't there to defend herself. All this speculation was based upon the size of a diamond and not rooted in any actual conversations with the woman about her career plans or ambitions. (For what it's worth, she did keep up the commute after she got married.)

Don't Hold Your Breath for an Invitation to the Wedding . . .

According to a survey by *Forbes* and The Knot, only 2 percent of women plan to invite their boss to their wedding, and 9 percent don't even tell their boss that they are engaged.[8]

Even as a CEO, I still encounter questions, spoken and unspoken, about how ambitious I really am, or should be, given that I am married. One of the most common questions I get as a CEO is the same question that recruiters asked of Anne: "What does your husband do?" In my case, the question behind the question is, "What does your husband do *that allows you to have such a demanding job?*"

My answer is multilayered and different for our family than it would be for anyone else's. I understand that people have a genuine interest in how others "make it work," so I try to give a detailed answer.* I don't mind sharing when people ask, but no one ever asks my husband these questions. I also can't help but notice that when people ask me if I can really handle the demands of my job alongside family and children, they ask with a skeptical or incredulous tone. I'm pretty sure I've been passed over for some job opportunities because of what people assume versus what I actually said about my ability to balance work and family.

---

* In my case, my husband has a demanding job, too, and travels even more than I do. My sister helps us care for our daughters, so I have the privilege of knowing that when they are not with me, they are in good hands with family. Beyond that, I schedule rigorously, I prioritize relentlessly, and I focus intensely on my children during nights, weekends, and vacations. Having a full and busy life energizes me and makes me a better wife and mother.

Jessica, a successful founder, CEO, and working mother, has felt at times that her job opportunities were limited by what others perceived to be her ability to balance work and parenting. "I had a CEO job interview where I felt like I was passed over for the opportunity because of how they viewed me," she shared. "They asked so many questions about my daughter, my home schedule, and what my husband did. After I made it clear I had made some money from selling my first startup, they asked, 'Don't you just want to stay home for a while?' It felt like they were trying to decide for me what I wanted and what I could handle."

Will she still travel? Can she take on a job this big? Will she have kids, and if so, will she return to work? These questions begin as soon as that engagement ring appears on the finger of a woman at work. Keep these questions in check. Don't penalize a woman now for the hypothetical maternity leave she might have at some point in the future. Give her the same respect you should give any employee regardless of gender: they come to work, you're paying them; assume they want to be there and will continue to want to be there. If you find your own supervisor raising these questions about a woman on your team, counter with an example of a woman you both know who didn't change her work patterns upon marriage or parenthood.

The assessment of a married woman's level of commitment to work centers on whether her job is the couple's top priority. A 2015 survey of Harvard Business School graduates found that 83 percent of married women made at least one major career accommodation for their husbands, such as relocating, reducing to part-time work, making a lateral move, or leaving the workforce altogether. But men make accommodations too; 68 percent of them, according to the Harvard survey.[9]

In my case, my husband and I have each made accommodations for the other's career. When he had a big job opportunity with Hyatt Hotels that required a move to their corporate office in Chicago, we went. I negotiated to adjust my job at Kaplan, which was not career-enhancing for me, but it wasn't detrimental either. Five years later, when I had begun my work with The Princeton Review, I had the opportunity to get promoted to the C-suite if we relocated back to New York. Chris left his job at Hyatt and searched for a new role in New York so that we could make the move.

It has always seemed kind of backward to me that we question the commitment of a woman once she gets married, on the basis that there may be less of an economic imperative for her to keep working. If she doesn't have to be here for the money, and is choosing to work anyway, doesn't that make her a more committed, more ambitious employee than a man who doesn't love his job but has a family at home counting on his paycheck?

"There's no match for the complexity of being a leader, mom, and wife. The amount of multitasking and work that goes into managing their lives is incredible," says Jonathan Grayer, who has led and invested in multiple companies led by women. "There's no need to say to her, 'This is a big job, can you handle it?' When a woman succeeds, you can be sure that she didn't get there without being very tough. You're putting a woman in a big job expressly *because* she's able to handle it."

Compensation: Pay People Based On Their Skills and Experience; Whether or Not You Think They Need the Money Is Irrelevant

When startup founder Megan was meeting with investors to raise money for her company, she often was asked if she planned to take a salary.

"I noticed that they would check for a ring on my finger when they asked that question," she recalled. In the cash-strapped world of startups, investors seemed to be pondering the possibility that she could save the company money by not drawing a cash salary, if she didn't really need it, and if she'd had a ring on her finger perhaps that would have signaled that she didn't need the money.

After working in investment banking, where she met and married her husband, Amy went on to work at a business magazine. She had one peer of equal seniority on her team. One year, she learned from this colleague that he had received a raise and now made significantly more money than her, despite her experience being slightly greater than his and her performance just as good, if not better. Fuming, she confronted their boss. He calmly explained that he only had enough budget to give one of them a raise, and since she was married to a banker, he felt the money was more important to her male coworker. While it's unusual that he actually admitted to it, it's unfortunately all too common for managers to think that way.

Another woman discovered that, following a broken engagement, it became easier to negotiate for compensation at her company. "Once they knew that I wasn't engaged, it changed the dynamic in our negotiations. Now they felt I was asking because I needed the money to support myself, whereas before I think it was perceived like I wanted more shopping money. When I was engaged, they acted like I didn't really *need* the money. I've actually been in a new, serious relationship for a while now, but I don't mention it around the office at all. I'd rather that they continue to think of me as my own breadwinner."

One man who worked for me used to bring up his wife every time he asked for a bonus or a raise. Based on his portrayal, he would be very happy working for free, but his demanding wife with expensive tastes always required more, and I would be putting his marriage at risk if I didn't help him out. These are some of the things he said to me in compensation discussions:

"I promised my wife I would ask."

"My wife wouldn't let me come home tonight if I didn't at least ask."

"My wife likes nice shoes and somebody's got to buy them!"

I imagine this could have resonated with a male boss who might be able to commiserate with his colleague about the burdens of supporting a wife. In my case, he probably should have thought harder about his audience, as I reminded him when I responded with a smile, "I like nice shoes too—maybe we can get a group discount." Men unapologetically use their wives and their responsibility as family breadwinners to ask for, and get, more compensation. Women likely won't be successful if they mimic this strategy and start playing up their needy husbands with luxurious tastes. Try to remember this dynamic and don't let the men who work for you get off easy by blaming their wives when they ask for a raise!

A Silicon Valley–based media executive champions another solution to equalizing the playing field in salary negotiations. "We had recently executed a pretty significant reorganization at our company, and one of the moves we made was the creation of an art department, which took teams from a few different areas and moved them together under a new manager, Cara. I sat down with Cara and her manager, who was also brand new thanks to the reorg, to discuss the new role. We talked about the vision for the team, key projects, strengths and weaknesses of the staff, and how she would get her current work done while also taking on management responsibilities. The best part came when Cara said, 'I feel like Sheryl Sandberg would be disappointed if I didn't bring up compensation.'

"With Sandberg's name, she navigated us to the topic of compensation. She broke the ice on what is typically a difficult conversation, and cut to the chase. I loved it."

So, if women can't use their spouses as a device for softening their negotiating asks, maybe they can use Sheryl Sandberg instead.

Position Eliminations: When Faced with Difficult Choices About Who to Fire, Leave Gender Dynamics Out of the Equation

Nobody likes to fire people—even people who aren't good at their jobs or who are in job functions that the company no longer needs. We're all human, and it's hard not to think about the personal implications of the decision. But when you make these tough decisions, it's important to be equitable.

Severance packages within the same company can look very different depending on who is getting them and how their managers handle it. In one example, a highly paid male executive had his job eliminated. He was married, his wife did not work outside the home, and one of his three children had very serious health issues. The board and the company made the decision to be generous in the context of his family needs, and they gave him three months' notice before his last day, an additional six months' salary as a severance payment, plus eighteen months of fully paid health-care coverage. At the same company, a female executive who was one level less senior but five years more tenured had her position eliminated the following year. She was single and healthy. She received two weeks' notice, three months' severance, and no incremental health-care coverage.

These are real dynamics that occur inside companies. Someone advocates to give extra months of severance or health-care coverage to a man because his family is counting on his income, or conversely a manager suggests that a company can save money on these same items when dealing with a single woman or a woman whose husband works, because she doesn't really need the extra coverage. Avoid the pitfall of offering overly generous severance terms to a man who has primary income responsibility for a family versus a woman who brings in a second income, is single, or is otherwise not financially burdened. It's not only inequitable, but people talk and increasingly will take legal action if they know that others received more generous terms than they did for seemingly equal work circumstances.

In the perspective of one CEO who has overseen multiple terminations, without a clear and consistent severance policy, it's difficult to be equitable in all circumstances. "You see all of these emotional considerations: hesitation to terminate a male who has a family to take care of, someone who is recently divorced, a family member with health issues. It's easy to fall in the trap of treating some people more generously than others," he says. "Only policy would have prevented that—a formulaic and generous severance package based on level and tenure, where the formula's the formula. The only variables are based on level and tenure, not what you think someone needs."

Even tougher are the situations where you need to reduce head count, say from two to one. One person stays and one person goes. Again, human nature is to pull in personal factors such as "He is really counting on this income" versus "She might not mind the break from working." If you've read this far, you know those are assumptions, not reality, and you need to let the work speak for itself. Don't choose based on who you think needs the job more. Not only is that unfair, it's discriminatory. You might think you're being a good human by considering the external life factors of each individual, but think about what you're doing to that woman who you think doesn't need the job as much. How much harder is it going to be for her to get rehired if others also assume that she doesn't really need the job? She may be competing with a male breadwinner, and others may again conclude that because he needs to work he must be more dedicated.

Stay focused on fair, fact-based questions: Who is producing the better work product? Who has the stronger performance reviews?

Who has the more fitting skill set for the future job that remains? That is the person who should stay.

Good Boss Checklist: What You Can Do to Be a Better Boss for Women

1. Don't let an employee's life event, such as marriage, change your perception of her commitment to the job.
2. Marriage does not immediately mean kids are on the way, so don't be like the relative at the wedding who asks when she will be bringing a bundle of joy into the world.
3. Pay her what she is individually worth, without taking her spouse's compensation or the size of her wedding ring into account.
4. Be careful about favoring employees who you perceive to need the income more when making hiring, firing, or compensation decisions.
5. Continue to give opportunities for travel, projects, and promotions regardless of what you perceive to be competing obligations at home.

To handle all these scenarios like a good boss, keep returning to a simple mantra: her marital status is not relevant to her career potential and her work product. Cultural and personal assumptions will creep into your view of the situation, and all you need to do to be a good manager is to spot when that's happening and to separate those assumptions from reality. Don't let a wedding ring impact your commitment to give her opportunities, pay her fairly, and support her career.

THE CEO PERSPECTIVE: BIG IDEAS FOR COMPANY-WIDE IMPACT

Knowledge Leaders: Script Recruiters with the Right Questions

Paradigm: Keep Recruitment on Target with Data

April Sarraille, the executive director of Knowledge Leaders, an executive search advisory firm, has seen enough pitfalls for women in the recruiting process that she designed a curated list of questions for her firm's recruiters to use to ensure that those initial screening conversations don't put women at a disadvantage. The questions are provided to candidates in advance to complete in a form so that they are not put on the spot.

"Women sometimes shoot themselves in the foot by offering up additional information and context beyond what's being asked. When I ask, 'How much travel works for you?' women will often go into their childcare situation, defaulting into explanations such as, 'My husband and I both work, but we have a nanny, and my parents live close by,' and so on," Sarraille shared. So she adapted her question about travel to be more specific and deliberate. Now she asks, "What percentage of time do you feel would be optimal for you to travel in this role?"

Similarly, she is careful not to ask about whether the candidate has a spouse, and if so, not to ask what that spouse does for a living. "We would never ask about a spouse's work, because it's irrelevant. The only time that I even bring in others is if the role requires a relocation, or very heavy travel, because those are things that impact the family unit," shares

Sarraille. "Ask, 'How would other decision makers in your family feel about that?' That is relevant—there are otherwise times when you get down to the eleventh hour and find that the high schooler doesn't want to leave in senior year, or the wife doesn't want to move. It happens not infrequently that it's not the candidate who's unwilling to move; it's the other decision makers." By no means is it only women who are limited by the work and preferences of their spouses; the opposite can often be equally the case. The important distinction Sarraille makes is to let the candidate offer up who that other decision maker is, being careful not to make assumptions or implications for them.

Finally, there's compensation, the stickiest topic of all. With shifting guidelines and legal restrictions, recruiters stay away from directly asking about a candidate's compensation history. "We have changed our approach to that over the last several years," acknowledged Sarraille. "I used to ask in the initial phone screen, 'What are you making? Base, bonus, options?' Now I don't even bring it up anymore. We are not allowed to ask. It's complicated; you want to lessen the inequality gap, and you want to be fair."

Knowledge Leaders' solution was to create an Alignment Questionnaire, which every candidate is given in advance of a phone screen and requested to fill out. Here are some versions of the compensation question asked in their form:

1. What level of compensation are you looking for in this role? Please specify both annual salary

and total cash compensation. (Do not include
your current compensation.)

2. As you consider compensation, what is most
    important to you, base salary, bonus, or (if
    offered) equity? (Do not include your current
    compensation.)

Carissa Romero, cofounder and managing director of
Paradigm, specializes in using company data to identify the
specific barriers to diversity, equity, and inclusion within
each organization's recruitment, hiring, and promotion
practices. She has worked with companies like American
Express, Etsy, and Lyft to implement data-based changes to
their programs.

Romero is a leading expert in fixed and growth
mindsets—people's beliefs about the nature of talents and
abilities. With Paradigm, she has designed a way to identify
human-based problems without making it personal. Data is
the bridge. The message is not, for example, "You are using
explicitly racist practices in your resume screening." Instead,
it's "We've analyzed the pool of resumes you received for
this job listing, and found that you are 93 percent less likely
to select a candidate of color versus a white candidate."

One interesting insight that Paradigm has found with
several clients is that the use of employee referrals can skew
toward less diverse candidate pools. "People tend to refer
people who they are most confident will be a fit for the company; people like themselves," Romero shared. Combine that
tendency with the fact that many HR teams don't even look at
resumes submitted directly through job listings if they have

a robust enough referral pool, and more diverse candidates aren't even getting considered. "Armed with this knowledge, companies can then make more proactive changes to their approach."

It doesn't have to mean doing away with referral hiring altogether. Romero continues, "At Pinterest, when we tried attaching a desired behavior to the referrals, we had a lot of success in getting a more diverse candidate pool. Just because an employee had first thought to refer someone like themselves didn't mean that when directly asked to consider diversity in their referrals they didn't have other qualified candidates in their network that would add diversity to the team."

The Big Idea

Standardize hiring processes to eliminate the potential for bias, leveraging data and standard forms and practices for recruitment.

Why It Works

- Takes potential for unequal execution of diversity goals out of the mix by scripting recruiting questions so that everyone gets asked the same thing, and in the same way.
- Calls out bias in action through nonpersonal data and statistics rather than making it personal by calling out individual behaviors.
- Data allows for clear goals and measures.

RULE #4

DON'T SIT IN HER CHAIR

eturning from maternity leave is a big day for a working mom. She experiences tremendous emotion leaving her baby at home, and she feels trepidation as she reenters the office. She worries about what or who might have moved in while she was out, to fill the space she occupied in her company. In my case, these fears turned out to be valid in quite a literal way.

On my first day back after giving birth to my first daughter, Marion, I woke up extra early. At three months old, Marion's timing was still pretty unpredictable. Some mornings she'd be up by six, but she slept in that morning. She was still resting peacefully at 8 AM when it was time for me to turn her over to my sister and go to work.

I really dragged out my exit from the apartment. I wasn't used to leaving the house in the morning anymore. I didn't want to leave before Marion woke up. So I kept stalling. *I can't remember if I brushed my teeth . . . I'll just do it again. I'm not sure if I parted my hair . . . let me go look. Did I put my keys in my bag? I should double-check.*

I finally made it out the door—to the stairwell of my apartment building, where I stood and cried for ten minutes before actually walking outside to go to the subway. On the F train, I avoided eye contact because I didn't want all those strangers to see my teary eyes, on the brink of spilling over at the slightest look of empathy. Fourteen stops later, I arrived at 57th Street and walked the four blocks from the station to my office. I had done this exact commute hundreds of times before, yet it had been months since the last time, so now it felt new again, more like a first day at a job than a return. I entered the building, rode the elevator up to the eighth floor, and took a deep breath as I walked into the suite. It was very quiet. I turned down the hallway, walked past my boss's office, saw that he wasn't in there yet, and approached the door to my own office, feeling that I had already accomplished a lot that day just by getting myself to this threshold. I went to sit down at my desk, but much to my surprise, someone was sitting in my chair.

One of my coworkers was seated comfortably at my desk. I scanned the office. His coat hung on the door hook, his books and papers were stacked on the desk, and his bag was on the floor. After exchanging greetings and making small talk about the baby, it became clear that we were both confused. I was wondering why he was sitting in my chair, and he seemed to be wondering why I was lingering.

"So, I'm back today."

"Yes . . . welcome back!"

"And . . . why are you in my office?" I asked, trying to maintain my good humor.

"Oh, well, I figured since you weren't going to be here for a while . . ."

"Oh sure, no problem," I said. We were still staring at each other, each expecting something different to happen. I tried again. "But now I'm back. So . . ."

"Oh!" he exclaimed, finally realizing that I was implying that I would need my office back. "Well, I'm all set up in here now. But my old office is all clear—actually, I moved some of your things in there while you were out."

Now, he hadn't just arbitrarily moved for no reason; he had traded up. His original spot, down the hallway, was smaller and darker than mine. I ranked above him in the company, so according to our workplace hierarchy, I was entitled to the better office.

"Umm, I don't remember agreeing to trade offices before I left," I continued, politely but firmly.

He realized that I wasn't backing down. "I mean, it's just an office," he said with a blend of condescension and exasperation.

I felt my face getting red. "Well, if it's just an office, then I'm sure you'll be fine going back to your own," I snapped, with very little control or graciousness.

Just an office?! If it was just an office, then why had he bothered to steal it in the first place? I was indignant. He left in a huff, and I stayed in a huff. I got my space back, but not without him making me feel like I was the unreasonable one. This was not a good start to the day. I had walked back into a turf battle and would soon realize that it wouldn't be my last.

"Why did I even come back here?" I muttered to myself.

The thing is, it wasn't just an office. That day, it felt like a physical manifestation of my greatest fear in coming back, that there was no place for me here. On an already emotional day, our standoff got me all worked up, and it made me feel like no one wanted me there.

I had always been committed to work. I had career ambition and held demanding, competitive jobs. I had gone to Harvard Business School. I had never contemplated *not* working once I had children. Throughout my pregnancy, I had rolled my eyes when people implied that there was even a possibility that I wouldn't come back. Yet here I was, less than an hour in to my first day as a working mom, already questioning whether I should stay. I didn't feel wanted or needed in the office, while I felt more wanted and needed at home than ever before. Contrasting my unwelcoming coworker to my adoring baby waiting for me, I felt pushed away from the workplace and pulled toward home.

According to the United States Census Bureau, 22 percent of women who work full-time up to and through a pregnancy either choose not to return to work or choose to leave within a year of the birth.[1] The time after the birth of a first child is the time when a woman is at the most risk of opting out of the workforce. At a time when she is feeling ever so essential at home and certain that her baby needs her, it is very difficult to return to a work environment feeling like maybe she's not as necessary as she used to be. For some, that crisis of confidence leads them to make the very rational decision to leave the workplace to focus their time where they feel wanted.

I've told the story of my stolen office many times over the years. I thought it was absurd, and I never really got over being angry about it. *Stealing someone's office while she's out having a baby? Who would even do that?* Well, it turns out a lot do it. My experience was not at all unique. Something like this happens to most women when they return from maternity leave. Typically, when I tell this story, at least one other person in the room will say, "That happened to me too!"

If you can count on one thing, know that while she's out of sight, office mates will feel quite free to raid her space and belongings. Staplers, pens, and extra phone chargers will get lifted. If somebody had an office chair with a broken wheel, they will trade it for "the good chair" in her office. If there was a hook she always hung her coat on, you can bet that someone else's jacket is hanging there now. Her space will become a storage room for all sorts of things—stacks of files, boxes, and bags. That is, unless her office is the nicer one, in which case someone will move right in. "I figured it was OK since you weren't going to be here for a while . . ." is a common excuse given. But no one ever really explains why, when someone is not using something for a few months, that means it's OK to permanently take it from her rather than give it back when she returns.

This problem is one of the easy ones for managers to fix: tell people not to take her stuff. And if they do borrow things, simply spend an hour the day before a woman is returning from leave rounding up everything to put back in its proper place. Don't make her fight for it. Prepare her space to be ready for her so that all she needs to think about when she returns is getting back to work.

Get in early on the first morning so that you can be present when she arrives to welcome her back. Help her feel that even though it is hard to have her new baby waiting for her at home, someone is waiting for her at work too. This can make the difference between getting her reengaged at work and pointing her on a path out of the workforce.

It's Not Just the Physical Workspace—It's the Work

As my coworkers started arriving for the day, they hugged me with excitement and welcomed me back. I started to feel my mood picking up again. But the greetings were brief; everybody else had work to do.

"I need to send an email out before my meeting, but let's get lunch later!"

"So much happened while you were out; we have to catch up, but I have a call starting—let's get coffee this afternoon!"

I watched them settling into their morning routines and jumping into meetings as I drifted. They were all so busy. I felt a burning worry: *They figured out how to get the work done without me for twelve weeks—maybe they don't need me after all.*

Stealing my office was the most literal way in which colleagues had encroached upon my space while I was out. But it wasn't just my physical workspace; there were more subtle ways that my place at work had been encroached upon. While I was on my leave and not there to defend myself, people had taken over my projects and were now trying to hold on to the good stuff and give me back only the least appealing parts of my job.

I noticed that for projects that seemed interesting and important, my colleagues clung to them upon my return, saying things like, "Well, at this point, it's already underway so I might as well keep it." Whereas for the thankless tasks, my coworkers were eager to toss those hot potatoes back to me. I returned to work to find my job downgraded by my colleagues. They said things that sounded nice, like, "I'll go to Australia—I'm sure you don't want to travel so soon after having the baby," or "Don't worry, I can handle the presentation to the CEO—I don't want you to feel pressured so soon after returning." But really they were trying to hang on to the most powerful pieces of what I had built into my role before I left it open to scavengers for twelve weeks.

My maternity leave came at a time of transition at my company. In the three months that I was out, we got a new CEO, and he in turn hired a new head of strategy, Garrett, who became my new boss. Upon joining the company, Garrett embarked upon a global review of every business that we had acquired in the previous years, to understand the reasons we bought them and the strategy for how we envisioned integrating each into the overall company mission. I had worked on every single one of these acquisitions, and I knew everything about the teams and business strategies. I was excited that such an important project had launched that was squarely focused on my area of expertise.

But on that first morning back, I learned that another new colleague, Nina, had been tapped to lead the global review while I was out. I discovered that she and Garrett were preparing to embark upon a trip to our Asia-Pacific offices to visit each business and spend time learning about their strategies.

"What's the schedule?" I asked. "I'll have to figure out travel plans."

"Oh," Nina said with a patronizing smile. "For budget reasons we think it only makes sense to have the two of us travel."

"If there are budget concerns," I said, "let's go through the list of what you're hoping to learn. I worked on the deals to acquire each of those businesses originally, so I've already been to all of these places. I spent weeks studying each of these companies doing due diligence, so I can probably cover a lot of what you're hoping to understand without anyone having to travel."

"The trip is already confirmed," she said firmly. "But while we're over there, we'll call daily to debrief you on what we're learning."

A week later, Nina and Garrett were off on their worldwide trip. In the first of the daily debrief calls, I listened with growing frustration and impatience as they told me things that I already knew about the companies. I cut Nina off, saying, "I already know all of this, so we don't need to spend time going through it now."

"But aren't you taking notes?" she asked. We were talking by phone, so I couldn't actually see her face, but I could hear the hint of a terse, forced smile.

"Taking notes?"

"Our work plan is to use these daily debriefs to summarize our thinking and learning so that you can document it."

"You're asking me to take notes? About the trip that you're on and I'm not?"

"Yes. In addition to what we cover on these calls, I'm going to scan and email you my handwritten notes, so that you can pull everything into one project document."

"So you want me to take notes on this call, and also retype your handwritten notes?"

"Yes, that would be great."

"No," I said flatly. "I'm not doing that."

Somehow, over the course of a three-month maternity leave, I had been reduced from a Harvard MBA leading and negotiating multimillion-dollar deals to a note-taker. *This was not my job*, I thought. My job was to evaluate investments and buy companies.

Much to the shock of everyone involved, I opted out of the project. There were a few other participants on the call from the New York office, and we were sitting together in a conference room circled around the speakerphone. After I declared that I wasn't going to continue working on the project, everyone fell silent and just stared at me. I stood up, gathered my things, and said, "OK, you guys can continue." As I walked out, I heard Nina ask through the phone, "Did she seriously leave?" I just kept walking.

My colleagues couldn't believe I had done and said what I did. But if I hadn't, I would have been allowing my job to get downgraded right before my eyes. I had lost control of my work during those three months that I was out of the office. That meeting was a turning point, after which I re-established my own lines for my work. Before I could move forward and upward in my career, I needed to fight to reshape and reclaim what I had before I had the baby.

At the time, I didn't have a good boss to advocate for me. My new boss was off in Asia, visiting with all the companies that I could have told him about, if he'd only asked and listened. Looking back now, I wonder how much easier it could have been if Garrett had fought some of those battles on my behalf, or better yet, stepped in to refuse to allow them to happen. He could have talked to me, gotten to understand my value, and made sure that I was positioned to do that work upon my return.

Instead, what I remember from those early months of working motherhood was a constant debate in my head: *Should I stay or should I go?* I vacillated between being determined to stay and setting a timeline in my head for when I would leave: *I'll work until the next bonus. I'll stay through the next maternity leave but that's it.* Instead of being all in during those crucial midcareer years, I was half in, half out. It's unlikely that a woman on your team will openly admit this to you, no matter how much she trusts you. Almost every woman has these debates in her head when she returns from maternity leave. Your job as a manager is to make sure that it doesn't become a self-fulfilling prophecy. Give her reasons to stay.

Understanding Her Perspective:
What a Good Boss Needs to Know

1. The first weeks back from maternity leave are stressful at every turn.
2. She is worried that she is no longer needed at work.
3. Seemingly small offenses like somebody stealing her stapler add up and feel significant.
4. She's being given a lot of reasons to stay at home and needs to feel like there are also reasons to go to work.

The work still has to get done while a woman is out on leave, so naturally people and activities creep into the space that she used to occupy. But too many women are left to their own devices to push their way back in and re-create that space. As a manager, there are things you can do to make this experience better for the women who work for you, and to make it more likely that you continue to retain them after they have children.

Women put a lot of planning and preparation into their transition to maternity leave. With nine months' notice, there is lots of time to think about what needs to be taken on and who can cover it. Projects are transitioned, instructions are left behind, cheat sheets are written to guide colleagues through where to find critical files and pieces of information. They want to ensure that everything runs smoothly while they are out, so they plan accordingly.

On the other hand, the return from leave typically feels a lot less planned. People continue to do what they've been doing for the past few months, without much thought put into how best to move work back. Instead, the woman has to go around asking and figuring out what work she can take back. A manager can take essential steps to do this better. Start planning in advance of her return, designate which work will move back to her, and who will handle that transition.

Offer check-ins during her leave in whatever format and frequency she'd like. Of course, leave is protected and she's under no obligation to take you up on the offer. But for many, it helps a lot to stay connected to work during those months and makes it easier to jump back into things when the maternity leave ends. I learned the hard way on my first leave how difficult reintegration into the workplace can be if you go cold turkey and don't check in at all. On my second leave I had weekly calls with my boss, and almost daily calls with my direct report.* Even if she doesn't want regular calls, often one-way communication can go a long way—sending her a weekly update email to keep her current on what's happening around the office.

Don't treat her as if she's gone indefinitely; always assume that she's coming back. Remember that most women do: 84 percent of women who are working full-time before the birth of a first child return to work immediately following a maternity leave.[2] So approach her leave coverage as having a beginning *and* an end. Too often, managers treat the return from maternity leave as if it is open-ended rather than planned. This means that a woman comes back to an environment that has been designed to function without her, but not designed to reintegrate her.

Treat the day of her return as thoughtfully as you would a new employee's first day. This reentrance into the workplace can make or break her post–maternity leave experience. Have a full schedule mapped out for her first day back. Ensure that her first week is full

---

* There's a lot of time to kill while out on stroller walks; I found that I enjoyed the mental stimulation of hearing what was happening in the office.

of meetings and that she is positioned to add value and feel valued. Give her back work that she was integral to before she went on leave. Schedule a meeting for her first morning back to go through the status of her projects with her and to ensure that she's productive from the start. Plan a lunch for you, her, and other colleagues. Keep her busy and make her feel essential.

Help her to jump right back into things. She is coming from a home environment where she was so needed that she couldn't even go to the bathroom on her own time. She's used to being of constant critical importance, and she wants to feel that way at work too.*

The Thing Nobody Likes to Talk About

There is another element of stress for women returning to work after childbirth, which relates to breastfeeding and all related functions. Many women continue to breastfeed for a few months after returning to work, sometimes more. During that time, they will need to pump breast milk once or twice during the workday, and oh boy is it stressful. Pumping creates multiple workplace challenges for women. They need to make time for it in a busy work schedule, and of course they can't just do it in the middle of a meeting. They have to deal with finding a private space to pump, and they need to plan ahead for the logistics of where to store the milk, how to commute with the milk,†

---

* That said, also let her go to the bathroom. Believe it or not, many working mothers talk about how the greatest perk of working life is getting to go to the bathroom when you want to, and without a child watching you do it!

† One time I literally cried over spilled milk. On my commute home, a container of my breast milk leaked and ran across the floor of a New York City subway car. It sloshed back and forth as we rode. I was horrified, and not because I was watching some poor guy unwittingly stand in a puddle of it, but because it took so much effort to pump, store, and transport it that losing an entire bottle of milk felt like pouring liquid gold down the drain.

and how to adapt all these systems when traveling for work. A whole chapter could be written on the expertise working moms develop in traveling with ice packs, securing minifridges in hotels, and creating makeshift solutions for doors that don't lock.

Most offices have some sort of lactation or comfort room for nursing mothers to use when pumping breast milk. Federal law requires that all employers provide all nursing mothers with necessary break time and an appropriate private space for lactation that is not a bathroom.[3] It does not necessarily have to be a permanent or single-purpose space; those requirements vary by state and are typically tied to the number of employees at the office location. That means that what was a conference room last month when there were no nursing mothers in the office could become a lactation room when a nursing mother returns to work.

During my own pumping trials and tribulations, I remember thinking to myself that the best training I'd had to prepare myself for those months in the office was from my older brother. When we were kids, we argued constantly. He was two years older than me, and I believe that he felt it was his mission in life to annoy me. One of his favorite things to do when I had a friend over, or just when I said that I wanted privacy, was to come into my bedroom and bother me. I made what I felt was a very clear sign for my bedroom door that read, "Private. All brothers keep out." He ignored the sign. So I started locking the door. He figured out how to use an unwound paper clip to pick the lock. I moved heavy furniture up against the door. He would push harder, slowly sliding the furniture back or tipping it over. Sometimes we just had a direct standoff, him pushing on the door from the outside and me bracing myself and leaning against it from the inside. I learned two things from this: (1) laying down on the floor and bracing your feet against the door holds it more strongly than pushing with your arms and (2) there is no real privacy in the world—even if you lock the door and put up a sign asking people not to come in.

When it comes to lactation rooms, coworkers often treat the designated nursing space as just another office or storage room, especially if they've had a stretch of time where nobody has been actively using the room for pumping. They try to get into these rooms, even if the doors are locked, even if you've put up a sign saying that you need privacy, and even if you blockade the door with chairs.

April, an executive recruiter, had her own challenges with pumping at the office early in her career.

"I worked at one of the big consulting firms in downtown San Francisco and they had recently set up a 'wellness room.' There were no windows, a bare-bones couch, and eventually a desk, docking station, and phone. I remember seeing a bike in there a couple of times and thought, *I wonder why that person doesn't use his own office.* He got the picture one day when he tried to get in the room to retrieve his bike while I was pumping. He started rattling the door and I'm thinking all I can hope is that the lock is strong," she remembers with a cringe.

It's very unsettling to have someone trying to open the door when you're in the middle of doing something private. When you're in a restaurant bathroom, door locked, another person might come along, try the doorknob, realize you're in there, and wait patiently outside the door. But other times, you get that person who doesn't just try the door once. They rattle it, shake it, push it, and don't seem to hear your voice through the door calling out, "Someone's in here." It's nerve-wracking because you really don't want them to walk in on you in the middle of a vulnerable moment. It also creates an uncomfortable interaction when you do open the door and walk out, coming face-to-face with the person who tried to break down the door while you were going to the bathroom. You might roll your eyes; they might look down or smile sheepishly. Ultimately, though, you can shrug it off and think, "Oh well, I'll never see that person again."

But in an office, you'll see these people again. Every day, in fact. A woman feels embarrassed walking out of the lactation room to face this person who tried to open the door because he knows what she was doing in there and she doesn't really want him thinking about her using a breast pump. And in that moment where she worries that he will actually succeed in breaking open the door, she is terrified because she really doesn't want him *seeing* her using a breast pump.

"He eventually pushed a note under the door about needing his bike," April continued. "Well, he had to wait for a response as, for those of you who have been there know, you aren't exactly mobile when pumping. When I did open the door, I found a young twenty-something guy overly embarrassed when I mentioned the lactation room wasn't for bike storage."

Pumping also creates a time constraint. It needs to happen, and needs to happen during pretty specific windows of time to maintain milk supply and to avoid discomfort, clogged ducts, and other painful things that men generally don't want to hear about. Most women are embarrassed about blocking workday time for pumping, yet they will physically suffer if they don't do it. A popular solution is to create fake meetings to try to hide it.

"I made up a series of entirely fake meetings with an outside consultant during the months that I was breastfeeding," reflected one executive. "I was not only a new mom, but I was new to my company. I was so busy every day that I realized that if I didn't block time on my calendar for pumping, I would get off schedule. At first, I set up daily recurring meetings on my calendar, twice a day for thirty minutes, once between 10 AM and noon, and the second block sometime between 4 and 5 PM. My calendar entries just said 'Milking.' I didn't think that anybody else could see them, obviously. Then a coworker kindly pointed out to me that our work calendars were shared, so basically everybody in the company could see when

I was pumping. So embarrassing. I could have changed my calendar privacy settings to hide my schedule information, but the company culture seemed to be big on sharing, and as I said, I was pretty new to the company and wanting to make a good impression. I didn't want to be a conspicuous nonsharer. I worried about people saying, 'Why does she have daily times that she marks private so that no one can see?'

"So, I decided that coming up with a fake meeting topic was the way forward. I figured people were less likely to ask me to move a meeting that was with someone outside the company, so I created a new series of recurring meetings with an external consultant. I even gave it a project name! I called it Project Jersey, as in Jersey cow. So every day I had 'Project Jersey Consultant' check-ins scheduled on my calendar."

Wouldn't it be better if women could just be honest about needing time for personal reasons such as breastfeeding, instead of feeling like they are leading double lives with fake meetings and vague explanations? These topics can be hard to address, but you need to make sure that your employees are comfortable asking you if they need to make allowances on their schedules, or if they need some private office space allocated. Just acknowledge that it's uncomfortable for her to bring it up, and help make sure that she gets the space and privacy that she needs.

Put Yourself in Her Shoes

An average of 273,000 women per month take maternity leave. In contrast, only 22,000 men per month take paternity leave. In simplest terms, that means women are about twelve times as likely to take parental leave. And while the number of women taking leave has been relatively stable over the years, the paternity leave count is up from 5,800 per month as measured just a few years prior. It always takes perception a little time to catch up to reality, so this means that in the minds of many, women are as much as forty-seven times more likely to take parental leave.[4]

This makes parental leave a woman's problem at work. When hiring a young woman, especially a recently married young woman, people speculate and worry about whether or not they are going to have to deal with her taking a maternity leave in the near future. That concern rarely surfaces for a young, recently married man because it's statistically unlikely that he will take leave, regardless of whether his partner has a baby anytime soon.

One of the greatest challenges to the ramp-up and equalization of maternity and paternity leave policies is that men don't take them, even when their companies offer equal benefits. Of men whose companies offered paid paternity leave, 69 percent said they were reluctant to take it because of the negative impact it could have on their careers. A male investor describes the dynamic this way: "If you're a young guy trying to make partner at a private equity fund, you're not going to put an auto-reply on your email saying that you're taking parental leave for twelve weeks. You're maybe going to take a week off when the baby is born, and then you'll get back to it."

Men can choose not to take the leave if they think it would be bad for their careers. But women don't have that option; as much as we talk about equalizing paternity and maternity leave policies, we can't ignore the reality that for women who have given birth, it is a necessary medical leave in which they are physically recovering from the birth as well as caring for their newborn. Leave for adoptive or surrogate parents tends to fall somewhere in the middle, with more days taken on average than for paternity leave, possibly because women and men both are taking this leave.[5] The only true equalizer is to make it so that everyone takes leave, whether it's physically needed or not.

#FunnyNotFunny Fact

Of men who take paternity leave, 90 percent report spending some of that time caring for the baby, and 80 percent report spending some time on household chores.[6]

What are the rest of them doing?!

When you factor in the lower percentages of women in management roles, and age factors, male managers have an even greater opportunity to endorse parental leave by not only improving the ratios of women to men taking leave, but to do it in the more visible role of a manager. The average age of a father of a newborn is thirty-one years old, whereas the average age of a mother of a newborn is twenty-six years old.[7] The average age of a first-time manager is thirty.[8] Taking all those statistics together, men have a greater opportunity than women to model parental leave in a management role. Stitch Fix CEO Katrina Lake said, "They always say culture comes from the top. The way you act as a CEO is going to reflect on how people at your company think that they should be acting. So if I see my job as one that I'm not going to take the full leave or I'm going to do a halfway thing or I think my job is too important to do it, the message I'm sending to others is that to be successful here they also should be forgoing their leave."[9] The same should be true for male leaders and managers.

Broader paternity leave has the potential to meaningfully improve the lives of working moms. It will lead to more men experiencing and normalizing the practice of taking time away from work to care for a newborn. Men can help remove the stigma from taking leave, and they can increase the expectation that the majority of people who take leave will return to work in the normal course. When Mark Zucker-berg, CEO of Facebook, publicly announced after his wife, Priscilla Chan Zuckerberg, had their child that he would be taking two months leave, he was acting as a good boss, modeling the behavior he hoped to inspire in other men, and normalizing the leave that women took.[10]

So many workplace challenges for women stem from the set-backs they encounter when they take maternity leave. Imagine how many of these dynamics would go away if everyone, male and female, took a new parent leave (or two, or more) over the course of their careers.

If all new fathers experienced this, too, maybe they would be more likely to treat taking twelve weeks off to care for your newborn as no big deal, instead of the possible career setback that it feels like now. Maybe people would stop thinking of parental leave as the first step toward an exit from the workplace, and instead view it as a nor-mal part of life that everyone does once or more over the course of a career.

Good Boss Checklist: What You Can Do to Be a Better Boss for Women

1. Prepare her work space for her return from parental leave, including taking back stuff that others borrowed.
2. Give her the option of checking in with you while she's on leave, so that the return to work doesn't feel so jarring.
3. Proactively plan for her return and create a full schedule for her first day back to help her feel busy and needed at work.

4. Respect, and ensure that others in the office respect, the private space needed for nursing moms.

5. Take maximum leave when you are a new parent, and encourage everyone on your team to do the same, regardless of gender.

THE CEO PERSPECTIVE: BIG IDEAS FOR COMPANY-WIDE IMPACT

The Knot Worldwide: Create Office Facilities Designed for Women

Wedding industry giant The Knot Worldwide (TKWW), which operates milestone planning brands The Knot, WeddingWire, The Bump, and more, employs more than 1,800 people. As part of its efforts to be an employer of choice, the company offers creative benefits designed to make life a little easier for the people who work there. With more than 70 percent of its employee base female, many of its employee programs are designed with women in mind.

The company's Bethesda, Maryland, headquarters is fitted with creative perks that address true pain points for working women. CEO Tim Chi knew that one area that needed to be tackled was the environment for nursing in the office. "My wife and other friends would tell nightmare stories about nursing at work: people having to hide in storage closets, paper over windows, figure out how to block doors without locks. It's a significant stress point for women. We had seventy babies in the company last year, so I knew it was important to our workforce and we needed to be intentional about designing something better. We wanted to create the Four Seasons of nursing rooms."

What they came up with was a spacious, purpose-built nursing room on every floor of the office, tucked away in a quiet corridor. These rooms have all the features that women wanted: doors with locks; sufficient space to feel relaxed, not cramped; ample refrigerator space; a sink equipped with the right tools for washing and drying breast pump equipment;

personal storage bins for each nursing woman; and a comfortable chair purpose-chosen for the task.

Each year the company's HR team identifies and evaluates additional perks. For example, they added a new benefit this year for nursing moms: access to a service called Milk Stork, which ships breast milk in refrigerated packs for women when they are traveling for work.

Another everyday challenge that TKWW's leaders heard from their teams was that there was never any time to get a haircut. It was one of those things that you keep putting off, and then when you finally have time to do it, you call your salon and can't get an appointment when you want one. So they opened Love Is in the Hair, the in-office hair salon at TKWW. Fully equipped with all high-end salon features, including a sink, stylist mirrors, and chairs, and Drybar blow dryers, it is available for all employees to come in to get their hair done, free of charge. It's another great example of a small way to make life a little easier for women by giving them one less thing that they need to fit into their overpacked schedules outside of work.

Not only do these benefits generate goodwill and loyalty from employees, but they can be a differentiator in recruiting and hiring as well. Multiple employee ratings on Glassdoor mention the "beautiful facilities," "calm and relaxed environment," and the "amazing perks—a hair salon!" When a company thinks about what women need from their workplace, it pays off in attracting and retaining great talent.

The Big Idea

Create thoughtful office facilities that are designed for women and solve for the things that make working life difficult for them.

Why It Works

- Reduces the everyday frictions that distract from focusing on work, solving logistical problems before they become fundamental workplace issues.
- Creates a tangible, visible demonstration that you see and care about who works for the company and what they need to be productive.
- Creates a competitive advantage by taking something that most workplaces treat as checking a required box and making it something where you are best in class.

WATCH THE CLOCK

t was around noon on a Wednesday, and a new email arrived in my inbox from the assistant to the CEO. The CEO wanted to meet later that day with me and a few others to review an investment proposal together. Could I do 5 to 6 PM that evening?

"Yes," I responded. "I can meet then."

I always relieved my nanny at 7 PM, which meant that I needed to be walking out the door of my office to head to the subway by 6:15 PM to ensure that I had at least a fighting chance of getting home on time. So long as the meeting ended by six, I would be fine. But when five o'clock rolled around, the CEO's assistant sent out another email saying that the CEO was running late, and that the CEO would let us know when he was ready to start. Then, five fifteen came and went, and five thirty was approaching. I went to my boss, who was also going to be in the meeting, and told him that I was worried it was going to run long, and that I really needed to leave by six fifteen to get home for the nanny.

"I wouldn't worry about it," he said casually. "I bet it won't take a full hour."

At five thirty the CEO was finally ready. We all filed into the conference room: me, my boss, and four other male executives, none of whom had primary childcare responsibility.

OK, I thought, *maybe we won't need a full hour, and even if we do, I can just run out as soon as we're done. Worst case, I will only be fifteen minutes late, and I can apologize to the nanny and beg for forgiveness.*

I held my phone under the conference table as I texted my husband frantically to see if he could get home in time as a backup. I kept checking my phone, but he didn't text back. The meeting was still going strong at six thirty and it appeared that the rest of the guys in the meeting wanted to keep going. I was too self-conscious to stand up and say that I had to leave. Nobody ever left a meeting with the CEO. Plus, I had a feeling that they would just continue without me, and then I would be left out of an important decision. I kept looking over at my boss to try to catch his eye, but he was engrossed in the discussion. He didn't seem to remember that I needed to leave, or maybe he didn't realize what time it was. I, on the other hand, was checking my watch every thirty seconds.

If I'd known at least a day in advance that the meeting would go so late, I would have made prior arrangements with my nanny to stay late, or I would have asked my husband to be sure to get home on time. But when things were unplanned and unanticipated, I was left in a bind. Childcare providers are not forgiving when you are late; they may love your children, but they are on the clock and have other places to be. Husbands, at least mine, are reliable when you ask them in advance to do something, but they don't usually assume primary responsibility for childcare on their own. Responsibility typically falls to women to either get home for their children or to make sure that somebody else is lined up to get there. As a manager, you should be aware that the more you let work run off schedule, the more you put women at a disadvantage.

The meeting finally ended at 6:50, and I rushed to gather my belongings and sprint out the door. I teared up as I sat on the subway,* feeling every moment of delay—every time we made a slow approach into a station, every time the train doors opened and closed. It felt like the world was working against me. I burst into my apartment at 7:40, apologizing as I dropped my things on the floor, and reached for Marion.

---

* If you've been reading closely, you'll realize that this is the third anecdote I've told that involves me crying on the subway. It happens, OK? I'm not ashamed to admit there are even more stories that didn't make it into this book. Ask me sometime about the guy on the A train who spilled scalding coffee on my lap and then fled at the next stop. For a laugh, do an internet search for "Reasons I Was Crying on the Subway," by *New Yorker* columnist Colin Stokes.

I sat down in the rocking chair and started rocking, more for my own sake than hers. My heart was racing and my face was flushed. I looked down at Marion and kept rocking. The way the nursery was set up in our tiny Brooklyn apartment, the rocking chair was over in the corner of the room. It had large wooden rockers, and as you rocked, the chair slowly slid back across the carpet, until it eventually ran into the wall and got stuck. You'd have to partially stand up, holding the baby in one arm while you used the other to shimmy the chair forward so you had room to rock it again. I did this over and over again, running into the wall at least fifteen times. Marion was drifting in and out of sleep as I rocked.

I got a text from my husband. "Hey just saw this! I'm grabbing a drink with Mike—do you still need me to come home?"

It was eight fifteen. His offer at that point was useless to me. "That's OK," I responded. "I'm home. Have fun with Mike."

I continued to rock as I wondered to myself: Was it really possible to be a good mom and be good at my job? I had felt so much stress over being forty minutes late. Who can live like this? What was just a routine meeting in the minds of those men elevated my pulse and my blood pressure to extreme levels and sent me spiraling into feeling out of control, helpless, and hopeless about my career prospects. All for what? Less than an hour's difference. This is the reality of how women feel the impact of time.

There were a few ways that my boss could have improved the situation for me. He could have said that the meeting needed to be at four instead of five. He could have moved it to the following day. He could have said at the start of the meeting that I would need to leave at six fifteen, so he wanted to be sure that I shared my thoughts first. He could have spoken up at six fifteen and told me I should go and that he would wrap up and fill me in. All those solutions have to do with time. Managers need to pay attention to the clock.

Respect the Schedule

Scheduling in advance, and sticking to the schedule, matters for the women on your team. With a predictable schedule, she can ensure that she's covering everything, but when things go off plan, it creates a domino effect on her other commitments. Of course, things *will* go off plan, both at home and at work. You can't ensure perfect adherence to a schedule, but you can make a difference by sticking to the elements of the schedule that you can control. Don't make last-minute changes on a whim, and don't stretch things outside of normal working hours unless absolutely necessary.

Switching a meeting from a 5 PM to a 6 PM start may seem like it's just asking people to begin and end a little later. But at the end of the workday, she's not just clocking out and relaxing for the rest of the night. She's likely to be tightly scheduled and needs to leave by a certain time. She needs to account for her commute and make it on time to pick up her children or to relieve a caregiver at home. If she has scheduled childcare to cover a nine-to-six day and you change up that last hour on her, she now has to beg her babysitter to stay late and pay extra for it, or if her sitter can't, then she goes through a series of calls or emails to find someone who can do her a favor. So, in moving the meeting time by an hour, you added to her workload, requiring time to be spent on redoing arrangements with her support system to accommodate that hour shift.

Early mornings are particularly hard to rearrange for a working mom, so don't ask her to come in early unless there's a really good reason and no other option. So much happens in the household in the morning—waking kids up, getting them ready for school, getting them out the door and transported to school or day care, and then allowing time for her commute to the office. Shifting that by an hour, or even a half hour, can cause major stress.

I still remember how I felt one morning when I had reluctantly agreed to skip my daughter Audrey's class breakfast to attend an 8 AM meeting. I arrived promptly, but the person who called the meeting failed to show up on time and didn't respond to emails or texts asking where he was. He strolled in at 8:40 and we watched through the glass walls of the conference room as he went to get a coffee before entering the meeting room.

"Oh, sorry," he apologized casually. "I forgot we had an early start today." I was internally fuming, so upset that I had let down my daughter for no reason, yet no one else seemed to notice or care.

For single moms on your team, the strain is even more pronounced. There will be many hours of each day when there is no backup in place for childcare; it's all on her. Remembering what time she needs to leave, and ensuring that the last meetings of the day end on time, will remove significant anxiety from her life.

Do Your Planning So That She Can Do Hers

There are times when something comes up last minute and there's nothing you could have done to anticipate it. But other times, it's you, the manager, who has the power to prevent last-minute changes, simply by planning ahead. The people who work for you are depending on you to let them know where and when they are needed. Often it can be known in advance; the only variable is when you as the boss will spend the time thinking through the plan.

Organization and planning do not come naturally to me. I'm a classic procrastinator. Left to my own devices, I don't really focus until I have to. Every three months, my company has a board meeting, four hours where I and others from the management team present business updates and strategic plans. The meetings are scheduled a year in advance, which gives plenty of time to plan. I set the agenda for the meeting, determine who else I want to present, and, based on that, who needs to travel for the meeting.

I have two working moms on my executive team who report to me. They start asking me a couple of months in advance of the next scheduled board meeting if I'm going to need them to come. The first time they did this, I got annoyed. I hadn't thought about what I wanted to cover in the meeting yet.

"I don't know," I would say dismissively. "I still need to figure it out."

Every few days, one of them would ask again. Each time, I was defensive. Their questions reminded me that I still needed to think through what topics to present, who I would need at the meeting, and what slides needed to be created. I saw it all as my work, and I didn't think about the impact it would have on them. I was so busy all the time. Why did they keep bugging me to start planning for a meeting that was weeks away when there were so many other things that needed to happen before then?

You would think, as a working mom myself, that it would have registered that they were trying to plan for their own family schedules. It was already blocked on my calendar, and my husband had marked the dates months in advance, so in my mind it was all set other than preparing the content for the meeting, which was my own work to do. It didn't register that others were waiting to plan their own logistics.

A week before one of these board meetings, I was on a video call with one of those women and said, "You know what, I think it would be good for you to present on this topic at next week's meeting."

"In San Francisco?" she said, and I could read the concern on her face.

"Oh, don't worry, it's not a big deal," I responded, thinking that she was worried about the actual presentation to the board. "We'll just use the slides you've already created; those are great."

"But do you want me to come?" she asked. "I didn't know you were going to need me there."

"Oh," I said, finally registering that when I asked her to travel, it created a domino effect of other tasks for her. She had a six-month-old daughter, and her husband had his own busy work schedule. "Let me think about this." If it could be a day trip, she just needed to make sure her husband was up for covering the early-morning and late-night hours until she got back. If she needed to come to the board dinner the night before, that meant at least one overnight, and probably arranging for extra help from her nanny. If it was longer than that, she needed to bring her nanny and daughter with her, since she was still breastfeeding. That meant extra costs: an extra hotel room, a plane ticket, and overtime pay for her nanny. I had unwittingly set off a chain reaction in her mind.

After thinking it over, I told her that I didn't think she needed to travel to the meeting. A few of the board members would be participating via video, so it wouldn't be unnatural for her to also participate that way. I said she was welcome to come, but that with the 8 AM meeting start it would require an overnight, and that I truly didn't think she would miss out on any opportunity by not being in the room.

Because I had created a system that worked so well for my own working mom needs, I had forgotten about how hard it could be for others. People were counting on me to give them advance notice to plan the rest of their lives, and I owed it to them to get myself organized as far in advance as I could when I was the one controlling the schedule.

Shift Changes Create the Biggest Hardship

"It was as if my employer completely disregarded the fact that I might actually have something other than work going on in my life," wrote a nurse practitioner when ranting in an online blog about the last-minute shift changes she endured as part of her job.[1] Your employees will feel disrespected and unhappy when you stick them with last-minute changes, and they will blame you for the challenges it creates for them at home.

But when the dynamics of last-minute planning are extended to the world of retail shift work, the implications can be dire for hourly workers, especially when they are working parents. Two-income households may be alternating day and night shifts to avoid the need for paid childcare. Single parents are likely towing the line of trying to line up paid childcare with their own schedules. In the world of retail, many workers are subject to unpredictable work scheduling, making it difficult to know what both their income stability and their childcare needs will be from week to week. These practices, which benefit companies by allowing them to match working hours to market demand, come directly at the cost of the employees.

The Second Shift

Any manager of women needs to understand the "second shift," a concept first introduced by professor Arlie Hochschild in her 1989 book, *The Second Shift*. In addition to their day jobs, working parents are doing a second shift of unpaid work at home, in the form of childcare, cooking, cleaning, and household planning. And women are doing a lot more of it than men. For many men, work is the only thing for which they bear primary responsibility. This is usually not the case for women, especially working moms. This responsibility translates into many hours of extra work. By Hochschild's estimate, it adds up to more than seven hundred excess hours of work for women in a year, an extra month of twenty-four-hour workdays. By another measure, after having children, a woman's household work increases by twenty-one hours per week.[2]

Women on your team have a lot on their plates outside the office. Not only does more household work in general fall on women, but more of the type of work that comes with time constraints. A father may contribute to the household by taking out the garbage, whereas a mother might be responsible for making lunches for the children. Taking out the garbage is not something that needs to happen at a certain time, or every day. Lunches, on the other hand, need to be made and eaten daily, and they need to be ready to go before the kids leave for school. All this work adds up. Single mothers bear an even heavier burden. They are working those extra twenty-one hours per week, plus they have to take out the garbage.

An Ohio State University research team added another twist: not only did it validate previous findings that women do more of the household work, but it found that men overestimated their contributions to the household and underestimated their wives' workload relative to the actual data gathered in the timekeeping study. So, even as men are making more effort to contribute at home more equally these days, the research suggests it's probably less than they think.[3]

The fact that she's working hard at home doesn't mean that she's working less than the men on your team. For better or for worse, the trade-off comes at the sacrifice of her leisure time. According to the US Department of Labor, men spend more time than women on leisure activities, including watching TV, socializing, and exercising.[4]

These tensions came to a head when the global COVID-19 pandemic disrupted the tenuous balance that working women had forged. Women had already stretched every minute of time available to get everything done. There was no room for error. Then childcare and education resources shut down, and with families spending all their time at home, household needs increased. Somebody needed to cook and serve every meal, load and unload the dishwasher (that seemed to fill up after every meal), and supervise the children. Something had to give, and what gave was often the jobs that women held outside the home. Primary responsibility for the increased household tasks predominantly fell to women, and when they couldn't keep up with the demands of work and home, they left the workforce. "My husband is not quitting his job . . . My kids are not dropping out of school," said one working mother. "So, what gives? Probably my work."[5] As a result, in the first three months of the pandemic, mothers with young children reduced their work hours four to five times more than fathers.[6]

Optimists believe that the experience of COVID will show more fathers the once invisible work that happens at home and will result in a fairer rebalancing of the workload. Employers and politicians have seen that access to affordable childcare is essential to the participation of women in the economy, and they are beginning to offer more support systems. If nothing else, the experience highlighted the reality that was already there: because women are balancing more external responsibilities, time matters more to them. This comes up at work in two key ways:

1. She feels a heightened need to make every minute count.
2. She has less flexibility to handle last-minute changes.

Working moms typically need to account for every hour of their day, and there is little margin for error. Be aware of what you're asking for and the underlying work it creates for her. If you do need to ask for a last-minute schedule change, don't then fail to show up on time or end when you said you would. In short, it's all about respecting her time.

Women are always watching the clock. But don't mistake that for a lack of engagement. I went out for drinks after work one evening with a few colleagues. When I said it was time for me to head home because I wanted to see the baby before she went to bed for the night, one of them asked me, "Do you feel like you always want to be two places at once now that you have a baby at home?"

I responded, "Actually, I'm way more focused now than I was before. I really enjoy the time I spend in each place so I'm not really getting distracted by one when I'm in the other mindset. The big change is that I've gotten really impatient about wasting time. I used to love a little office chit-chat and I didn't mind so much if things were running late. But now I feel like everything I do needs to be purposeful; I don't have time to waste."

Many women I talk to share that feeling. We love working, and we love parenting, and we can do both as long as we can use our time wisely and with purpose. You will be a good boss if you can help her make the most of every minute she's in the office and help her get out on time to start her second shift.

Embrace Multitasking

The jury's still out as to whether women are actually any better than men at multitasking.[7] There has been a tremendous amount of chatter on the subject, declaring clear but conflicting conclusions: Women are natural multitaskers. Men are better multitaskers. Multitasking is worse than having one-track focus.[8] Whether or not women are superior at quickly transitioning back and forth between tasks, what we do know is that they don't have time to sit idly. There's no time for relaxing!

I once worked with a woman who would bring her knitting to our meetings, and initially I was offended by it. I interpreted it as a confrontational statement intended to convey that she expected

Understanding Her Perspective:
What a Good Boss Needs to Know

1. Time is a valuable commodity for her. Everything is a trade-off, and every minute counts.
2. Last-minute changes stress her out because she needs to live by a schedule.
3. She's cautious about speaking up about time restrictions because she doesn't want to look like she's not committed.
4. She's working hard at times and in places where you can't always see it.

to be bored and needed to bring along extra entertainment. I said something to her manager about it and learned that she always did this because multitasking helped her to feel more engaged. Once I understood her perspective and her need to feel constantly productive, it made a lot of sense. And it certainly didn't hold her back from being an active, valuable participant in discussions.

As a manager, you have lots of opportunities throughout the day to support your team's productivity. For example, if it's possible to work through lunch so that an all-day meeting can end at 5 PM instead of 6 PM, that can make a big difference. Fewer large-group meetings and more targeted breakout sessions with only the people needed to drive the decision or action will help reduce idle time too. Talk to your team about their preferences, and you likely will find that women are all about maximizing productivity, which means doing two or more things at once whenever possible.

Sometimes Less Is More

A good boss understands that face time or constant availability is not the only way to work hard. Women are power users, trying to concentrate their work into fewer, higher octane hours. A manager should embrace that and see the value they are getting out of the bargain, rather than thinking that the only way to be dedicated to work is to be always working.

We work to fill the time we have. Never was this more true than in my first job in investment banking, where twenty-hour workdays were the norm, and it wasn't acceptable to be seen leaving the office before 10 PM. But were we really more productive than someone who stayed focused, worked intensely across all their dedicated work hours, and left at six o'clock? It's doubtful. We certainly took a lot of coffee breaks, dinner breaks, gossip breaks, and workout breaks, knowing that no matter what we did we would have to stay in the office all night anyway.

Women suffer from the perception that they are working less hard because they are spending more time on their children. So, if a woman on your team wants to work fewer hours but she works them more intensely, give credit for that. You're likely getting more than your money's worth in productivity.

"The women who work for me often take a different approach to working hours," shared Drew, CEO of a large organization with an executive team that is more than 50 percent female. "They're more likely to say, 'I have to be home at five thirty to relieve the nanny, so I'm going to really crank until then.'" He also often finds that women with kids go back online after the kids are in bed. "That's certainly not required, but I love that," he shared. "If you want to work an hour from 8 to 9 PM instead of from 5 to 6 PM, more power to you."

Encourage Everyone to Be Open About Their Obligations Outside of Work

As we covered in Rule #2, talking about your commitments outside the workplace serves to cultivate higher-quality relationships with your colleagues by connecting on the things that matter to you. But it can also serve another purpose: to make others less self-conscious about having to attend to personal things during standard working hours. After years of working in environments where nobody really admitted when they stepped away from work for a personal obligation, I experienced a very different atmosphere when I went to work at Tutor.com. It was entirely normal to hear in a team meeting that someone was dialing in late because she had to take her daughter to the doctor, or for someone to give a heads-up that she wasn't going to be in the next day's meeting because she had a parent-teacher conference during that time slot. No doubt, a primary reason for that was that there were more working moms on the executive team. But we all talked about what we had going on at home, men and women both. Everyone took liberties to adapt our work schedules to fit our parenting schedules. I felt so much more comfortable in that environment because everyone was honest.

Before I was at Tutor.com, I would discreetly block "meetings" on my calendar for those types of events, and keep my fingers crossed that no one would ask me about them. I would say, for example, "I have a lunch meeting," not specifying that the lunch was at my daughters' school. I hid all of it from people because I didn't want to look like I wasn't 100 percent dedicated to work, all the time. This practice of creating false meetings is common among women trying to hide the reality that sometimes real life happens during working hours. As covered in Rule #4, the strategy is often deployed by breastfeeding women during working hours. But it continues to happen far beyond those years.

After having her first child, Molly, an advertising executive, reduced her client list down to a single dedicated account. She was giving that one client the same amount of time and attention as always, but because she no longer had any others it allowed her to reduce her schedule and pay to part-time. Yet for a full year after she made that change, she didn't tell her client that she was only working part-time for her agency.

"I was terrified about his reaction, that he would think I couldn't cover all of his needs," she said. "So I never said anything. On Mondays, for example, I didn't work, but if he emailed me I would just write back with a few hours' lag and say, 'Sorry, I was tied up.' If he emailed on a Sunday, I would put the kids in front of the TV and do the work on my laptop. He never realized the difference."

If everyone, men and women alike, just talked more honestly about the things they make room for during the workday, employees wouldn't feel the need to apologize or hide whenever they need to adapt a schedule for a personal obligation. As a manager, think actively about creating an environment where women feel comfortable being honest about what they need to do and when they need to do it.

Work Doesn't Always Have to Happen Between Nine and Five

Being a good manager requires not only flexibility, but trust. Employees understand that flexibility is a two-way street and that it's earned, not automatic. As long as the work is getting done, a good boss will focus on the work product itself, and not on when and where the work is happening.

Everything is a choice when it comes to time. Someone can choose to work on a project from 10 PM until midnight so that he can take a couple of hours in the afternoon to go see his son's school play. My teams know that they can generally catch me on email from 6 to 7 AM, but good luck catching me at eight thirty, when my phone's tucked away in my bag while I mingle with other parents at school drop-off. Everyone does it differently, and the best thing you can do as a manager is to model your own balance and choices openly.

A single mother with a long commute and strict day care hours shared her frustrations with me about her manager's inflexibility. She had asked for, and received, accommodations, including two days per week to work from home, reducing time lost to commuting. On the days that she did come to the office, she arrived later and left earlier than the standard office hours. This didn't mean she was working any less; she worked diligently through her long bus commutes and was often back on her computer after her son's bedtime, working until midnight or later.

Yet one day, upon seeing her return from her lunch break with a shopping bag on her arm, her manager questioned her productivity. Why was she shopping in the middle of the day? There was a perfectly good reason. She had run out at lunchtime to pick up a costume that her son needed for school the next day, and she had grabbed a salad on her way back to the office, which she now planned to eat while she worked. In that moment, she felt mistrusted and undervalued. "He shouldn't have to see me working to believe that I'm working hard. I'm getting the work done, and that should be all that matters."

There are times when something has to happen at a certain hour, but also times when it doesn't matter. Individual contributor roles might not require more than a few scheduled hours per week for team and manager interactions. Any role, all the way up to CEO, has some element of independent work: time spent emailing, reviewing, analyzing, and producing. Much of that can be done at 5 AM or 5 PM—it's all the same. So much of family life happens around the child's schedule, which often directly conflicts with standard work-ing hours. It might be absolutely critical for a woman to be with her child from the hours of 6 to 8 PM, but she might then be very happy to sit down at her computer and work for a couple of hours after the child's bedtime. Where there is flexibility, let her use it, and don't get hung up on which hours she's working.

Flexible Hours Doesn't Have to Mean Part-Time

After having her third child, Kimberly, a senior vice president at an investment fund, felt that she needed more flexibility than her demanding job allowed, but she loved the work and didn't want to walk away from the reputation and value she had established for herself in her career. She was the most senior female professional at her firm and had spent years working day and night, even after having three children. She went to her fund partners with a proposal that would reduce her work to 65 percent of regular hours, including three days per week in the office, in exchange for taking a 35 percent pay cut.

A year into the new arrangement, she reflected on how it was going. "Well, I'm still working more than forty hours in a typical week, but I'm able to be more assertive in fitting it in to my schedule. Not having to go into the office every day is huge, and I'm definitely able to be present for more events with the kids. But . . . I think I've put myself at a disadvantage for making managing director by cutting back my time. Of course, I haven't been able to actually cut back hours nearly as much as my pay cut would suggest—I'm still working more than a normal full-time job and just not getting paid nearly as much. I'm starting to realize that the men in the office just take the days out of the office or leave to go to something for their kids or golfing or whatever, without apology. And they certainly don't offer to take a pay cut. It's possible that I served up a structure that allowed them to pay me less for equal work, and now I'm a great value for them."

Many professional firms offer up similar structures, in the name of helping working moms achieve the elusive balance between having a challenging career and flexible time for their families. The idea goes, if you could keep your great job but only be responsible for half the work, you can work hard and love your job for part of the week and spend the other part with your children, stress-free and unapologetic about taking that time away from the office. Elite firms offer career paths for women who want to reduce their schedule after having children, or formal "job share" programs where two women split a single professional role.

These "solutions" don't always work. High-achieving women tend to give more than their allocated share of time to the job, and they are left feeling underpaid because they've agreed to take a partial salary but aren't actually working partial hours. Opportunities to advance are also taken from them because they have self-identified as someone who is willing to pare back work responsibility and income to care for her family.

Flexibility is a great tool to allow working parents to have rewarding careers while also being present for their families. But childcare is a full-time job, and work is a full-time job. There are cases where people constrain their work availability in the name of flexibility, and managers need to know when and how to set limits in a fair and consistent way. Consider the case of someone who wants to consolidate all meetings during school hours and have only individual contributor time after 3 PM. Depending on the job and the age/demands of the children after school, this can work. But it doesn't work if the job sometimes requires meetings to be held after 3 PM, if the work can't be done remotely, or if the employee can't really focus on individual work once the kids come home.

My advice to both managers and employees is to be honest about what you want, and clear about how it is working. If someone wants to work from 9 AM to 3 PM and then also add in two hours early in the morning or late at night, it's agreed with the manager, and the full-time workload is getting done, there's no reason that can't work. But if what they actually want is to only work from 9 AM to 3 PM, you should call it that.

Men are typically more comfortable, and less apologetic, about taking the time they need for family without sacrificing their position or income at work. Years before the COVID-19 pandemic, I encountered an early experiment in work from home combined with full-time childcare responsibility, conducted by a man who had worked at our company for years before having children. He was always reliable, and always in the office. I noticed at some point that I hadn't seen him in a while, and I asked his boss if he had left the company. She got an uncomfortable look and said that his wife had recently had a baby.

"Oh!" I replied with enthusiasm. "I feel so badly that I didn't know. So he's taking some time off to care for the baby?"

"No, he's working. He's just also watching the baby full-time, so he needs to work from home now," she explained, kind of quickly.

"Hold up. He's the full-time caregiver?" I asked skeptically. "Permanently?"

"Yes . . ." she responded.

"In my experience, caring for an infant is a full-time job, and working for us is another full-time job. The two are typically mutually exclusive. Is he really able to get it all done?"

I believe that as long as the work gets done, we should support flexibility. I wanted to apply that philosophy to this situation. But in this case, I wasn't sure that the work was getting done. I asked questions about his performance, participation in meetings, responsiveness, and general availability. Not surprisingly, the answer was that his new full-time caregiver gig was a major hindrance to getting his work done for his day job. Under the surface, there were complaints about missed deadlines, less productive remote interactions, longer response times, and conference calls interrupted by a crying baby. His job had been office-based, and his manager hadn't discussed with him whether or how it would work to shift it to 100 percent remote. It just kind of happened because he didn't ask; he just did what worked for him.

It wasn't adding up, and the work wasn't getting done. We had to make a change. Ultimately, his manager gave him the choice. He could arrange for childcare and keep his full-time job, or he could resign to spend time as a full-time caregiver. He resigned.

Consistent rules about work flexibility set us up to be able to see clearly and act fairly when the work wasn't actually getting done. But there was another lesson in this experience for me: men don't ask for family accommodations; they just take them.

In this case, the employee managed to take a full-time salary for six full months before we made the change. In an equivalent situation, I believe most women would have asked to extend unpaid maternity leave before anyone would have tried what he did. Just look at all the women who exited or reduced working hours during the COVID-19 pandemic because they recognized that without childcare, they could not manage a full-time workload. The best practice lies somewhere in between. Managers and direct reports should discuss and agree on all flexible working arrangements. If things are working well, employees will feel comfortable asking for the flexibility they need, but they will also feel a responsibility to prove that they can get the work done in the new format they are proposing. In those scenarios, no one has to make concessions.

Good Boss Checklist: What You Can Do to Be a Better Boss for Women

1. Start and end meetings on time.
2. Don't schedule meetings outside of standard working hours, unless it is absolutely necessary.
3. Give as much advance notice as possible for travel, schedule changes, or early/late meetings.
4. Treat time as valuable and support multitasking.
5. Don't get hung up on which hours are for work or personal time when flexibility is possible.

THE CEO PERSPECTIVE: BIG IDEAS FOR COMPANY-WIDE IMPACT

Hello Products: "Stress-free" Flexibility

Lauri Kien Kotcher, the CEO of Hello Products, a fast-growing oral care company that brought charcoal toothpaste to the masses, set out to establish truly stress-free flexibility as not just a part of working life at Hello, but as a core value. In her prior work as a partner at consulting firm McKinsey & Company, Kien Kotcher had successfully navigated her career as a working mom despite the stress and challenges of managing her home schedule and work schedule. At Hello, she set out to build a company that was designed to allow its employees to succeed by removing that stress.

No company can completely eliminate the stress that arises from having to manage a sometimes-overwhelming amount of responsibility that comes from the combination of job requirements and household management requirements. But Kien Kotcher identified a third generator of stress: the need to hide, explain, or apologize when an employee needs to do something for her family at a time that she is also expected to be at work. The common response to this stress is to lie, either outright or by omission. Instinctively, many women will try very hard to avoid saying that they have to leave at five o'clock to make it to day care on time, or they will say that they can't meet at 11 AM because "they have a conflict" rather than admitting that the conflict is a doctor's appointment for their child.

So, at Hello, a foundational rule is that everyone leaves when they need to leave, no explanation and no apology. "We tell our employees, you are 100 percent supported in the way you choose to manage your life," says Kien Kotcher. If you need to leave on the early side to make it to day care pickup on time, you do it. If a child stays home sick from school and you need to work from home that day, you work from home.

But doing this well requires conscious flexibility rather than total flexibility. "We set a default expectation that we prefer to have everyone in the office together on weekdays from nine to five. It's important for collaboration and trust that we spend time together." So it's not a case of work whenever you want, wherever you want. Kien Kotcher knows where employees are, and if they are not in the office, she generally knows why. In fact, she was able to rattle off a list of specific scheduling needs for every member of her own team. It's just that she is imminently clear that family obligations are a legitimate reason not to be in the office, so when they come up, employees know that they can do what they need to do without apology. This trading of one type of flexibility for another is what allows for truly no-apology family flexibility without disconnectedness. Culture drift can come when a team is too flexible or remote and the members are not getting reliable time together to interact and solidify their connections to each other and to the company. What's unique about Hello is that they accomplish one type of flexibility partly by reinforcing another core expectation that all employees be in the office during standard working hours to facilitate collaboration. There is a general understanding that work happens together in the office as much as it can.

Another way that Hello creates stress-free flexibility without sacrificing organizational productivity and growth goals is by establishing a clear expectation that working hours are traded, not reduced, in the name of making room for personal needs. Meaning, just as the executive team respects that its employees' family obligations will intrude upon traditional working hours, employees respect that, in turn, work obligations will intrude upon traditional family hours. If someone leaves early every day to pick up their kids, no problem at all. But they likely need to find some time later that night to go back online and finish up what they left in motion when they left the office that day. And, just as a child's school may call at one in the afternoon and it just can't wait, sometimes the opposite happens and Kien Kotcher needs to send a text at nine at night to get a time-sensitive answer. The key is that both are OK and nobody needs to hide or apologize when work and home needs blend, mix, and overlap.

Kien Kotcher designed Hello's model based on an eye-opening moment in her own career history, while she worked at McKinsey & Company. After having children, Kien Kotcher shifted to their part-time consulting track, working four days per week. She became the first person in McKinsey's history to make partner from the part-time track. Once she did, the demands and expectations of the partner role made it more and more challenging for her to contain her work to her four-days-per-week schedule. Work was increasingly infringing upon her nonworking days, and the total amount of work was expanding. In a conversation with a male colleague, who was also a partner, she discussed her struggle to reconcile her expanding workload with her knowledge that there were going to continue to be family needs during working hours. The part-time schedule just wasn't working. "He said, 'Why don't you just do what we do?' meaning why don't you do what men do," Kien Kotcher recalled. "Work full-time, and just go when you need to go to deal with family things. Everybody has things come up that pull them into family stuff during the workweek; you just make it up on your own time later."

That realization prompted Kien Kotcher to shift back to a full-time work schedule, and in doing so, she found she could manage her life better than she could when trying to force all work into four days and all family responsibility into the other three days. Life just doesn't work like that. This alternative model says the answer for some professional women is not to reduce their responsibility, and their pay, to part-time. The solution is to keep them on a full-time career track but to be a company that understands and allows them to take a modern approach of blending life and work into whatever works best for their schedule. Not every job fits into a perfectly predictable four-day, or five-day, box. At Hello, they've found a way to allow their employees to let work and family overflow into each other's boxes with no apology, penalty, or shame.

The Big Idea

Institute a policy of stress-free, no-apology flexibility.

Why It Works

- Lets employees determine how they manage their work and family obligations.
- Accepts that just as work blends into family time, family blends into working hours.
- Removes the stress employees feel about explaining and defending the decisions they make about where to be and what to do and when.

SPEAK UP SO THAT SHE DOESN'T HAVE TO

At age twenty-three, I was a young investment banker, and found myself out to dinner one night with colleagues at a fancy steakhouse. The mood was lighthearted. Two weeks prior, we had flown from New York to London to pitch a deal to a client. On the spot the client said they not only wanted to do it, they wanted to do it right away. So we ripped up our return flight tickets* and stayed on for two weeks, working around the clock. On this last day, after finalizing the deal, we went out for a celebration. I had enjoyed working with the team, and there is a special kind of bond that comes from working nearly twenty-hour days together, away from our friends and family back in New York. I was looking forward to a decadent meal that was sure to include fancy bottles of red wine and expensive food, the kind that I would never pay for on my own dime.

As the only woman seated at a table in a private room with eleven men, I was an anomaly for sure. I was also the youngest person at the table. The waitress kept shooting me sympathetic looks. My boss on this project—we'll call him Nathan—was planted at the center of the table, holding court. I didn't really know him. He had joined the firm from another investment bank only a few days before we had flown to London. When a lunch delivery had come to the office earlier in the week, I had offered to pay, saying, "Oh, do you need me to get it? Your corporate card probably hasn't come through yet." I genuinely meant to be helpful, but he was furious. He scoffed at me and snatched the receipt from my hand. "What are you talking about, Kate? I'll get the bill." I didn't realize that it would undermine him in the eyes of the client and the lawyers to be so new to Goldman Sachs. It was only later, after midnight that night, when Nathan and the other more senior team members had left us to keep working, that one of the

---

* This was back in the day so yes, we had paper tickets.

lawyers said to me, "So the paint's not dry on Nathan's office yet, huh? It shows." Then I understood—he didn't have the experience yet to back up his big talk, so he was kind of bluffing on the job.

Getting this deal was a big win for him, a way of coming in fast and showing he could be a rainmaker for the firm. Needless to say, he was therefore in a good mood at this dinner, on the day we got the deal done. I was in a good mood too. Until he looked across the table at me, and called out, "Hey, Kate, do you have a boyfriend?"

Inwardly, I groaned. This was not the first time I'd felt singled out in a business setting. Working in investment banking, I was often the only woman in the room. I could frequently feel an unspoken tension, where I could tell that the men were acting differently, or curating their conversations, simply because I was there.

I had become increasingly self-conscious about this dynamic, and I just wanted to be "one of the guys." I would try to find small ways to seem less different. For example, when I started my investment banking career, I didn't eat red meat at all. Yet here I was, less than two years later, ordering a filet mignon, medium rare. It was simply too conspicuous at those fancy dinners not to order a steak. Everyone would notice and turn their eyes on me. "Chicken? At a steakhouse?" "Are you sure you don't want a steak?" I couldn't change that I was a woman, but at least I could reduce other differences.

When Nathan turned the attention of the table to me, I tried to balance my smile to be polite and friendly, but not suggestive. I had to be so careful about how I looked and sounded: my words, my tone, my smile. It was like trying to defuse a bomb. "No," I responded carefully. "I don't have a boyfriend."

"Great. Tell us a good story—you must get hit on all the time," he continued.

"Oh, not really," I said neutrally. "I'm working all the time; I don't even have time to go out." I didn't want to seem uptight, but I also didn't want to encourage him. So many situations for women require extra thought on her part to choose the right words to maintain this delicate balance.

The conversation then shifted to the topic of cigarette smoking, which in 1999 was starting to be less popular in increasingly health-conscious New York, but it was still very common in London. Nathan again turned the conversation to me. "What about you, Kate? Do you smoke?" he asked.

"Actually," I replied honestly, "I've never smoked a cigarette in my life. I grew up with my mom smoking two packs a day and saw what she went through when she quit. So I swore I'd never start."

"Oh, I'm disappointed," Nathan declared, speaking to the table. "Can't you guys totally picture Kate in, like, tight leather pants, smoking a clove cigarette?"

At that point I couldn't even muster a fake smile. I blushed heavily (I'm a blusher) and looked down awkwardly at my plate.

One of the lawyers, the senior partner on the team, spoke up in a good-natured tone, "Nathan, as your lawyer, I advise you not to say things like that." Everyone laughed and the conversation moved on. It strikes me now that I owe that man more gratitude than I realized at the time. In a moment when all eyes were on me and I had no power to change the circumstances without drawing even more unwanted attention to myself, a more powerful man—who had no obligation to act, but also nothing to lose—jumped in to put a stop to the conversation. He was able to say it and have it roll right off him, whereas if I had spoken up for myself, it would have become "a thing."

Don't Invalidate or Minimize the Discomfort a Woman Experiences

Nathan's words, and the attention they brought upon me, had bothered me, and it made me uncomfortable around him. When we got back to New York, I went to my staffer, the person in an investment banking group who manages the work assignments of the analysts. I told him the story and asked not to work with Nathan anymore. The staffer was very nice about it, but he gave me the advice not to make a big deal about it by asking to get taken off the team I was already on. He said he wanted to keep me on that one team, but that he would make sure not to put me on any future projects with Nathan. He also recommended that I not mention the story to anyone else because he felt it would make others nervous to work with me if they saw me as a "complainer."

I took the advice and continued to work with Nathan, trying to avoid direct interactions as much as possible. I internalized the advice that my staffer had given me, and from that point on, as I encountered slights, awkward situations, and uncomfortable circumstances that I believed were due to my gender, I kept them to myself or only shared privately with a close-knit group of female colleagues. They all did the same. We wanted to fit in on Wall Street. We knew that nobody liked a complainer, and in an environment that had mostly men, we knew it mattered that they like us.

No one even spoke to Nathan about his behavior. My staffer told me it was for my sake because it would be obvious that the feedback was coming from me and they didn't want Nathan to hold it against me. It left me on my own in an imperfect situation, figuring out how to find an acceptable, if not optimal, resolution for myself.

My staffer told me that he was sure it was just a case of Nathan being unaware of his impact; he couldn't imagine that Nathan's words were meant to make me uncomfortable. How he could be so sure, when he hadn't actually spoken to Nathan about it, is unclear. With every statement made, there are two sides: intention and impact. If the recipient of a remark feels it was sexist, but the speaker says that wasn't his intention, is it sexist? Do we judge by intention or impact? Managers, or coworkers, often excuse or minimize the words of a colleague, saying, "I don't think he *meant* it that way." To me, that's an easy way out. Intention shouldn't trump impact. If a colleague says something to a woman and she thinks it was sexist, listen to her. She's in a way better position than anyone else to know how the comment or action felt to her, so you should respect her view. Instead of dismissing the impact on her by saying, "I didn't mean it that way," it's always better to acknowledge the impact by saying, "I'm sorry; I didn't realize and I won't say it again."

A situation in a first-grade class raised similar questions of intention versus impact. One girl, who was white, told some other white girls that they should all be friends, but that the girls with brown skin should be in their own friend group. As soon as a parent caught wind of this, it was reported to the teachers, counselors were brought in, parents were notified, and a necessary conversation about race exploded in and around the class. Two parents, both white mothers, were chatting about the situation. One parent tried to give the young girl the benefit of the doubt.

"I'm not sure it was *racism*—I think she is young and thinking about social categories and misapplied some lessons."

The other mother, who is married to a Black man and has biracial children, said, "You know, I used to think that way and give people the benefit of the doubt. But my husband, who has much more direct experience with racism than I ever will, strongly believes that when these things happen, they are what they sound like. He believes it's actual racism, whether intentional or not. If you aren't in the afflicted class, you can't really make a judgment that something isn't offensive; you just don't know what it feels like."

That same lesson applies to gender-loaded comments in the workplace. If you are not a woman, you don't know what it feels like. If she says it makes her feel uncomfortable, it makes her uncomfortable. Period.

Understanding Her Perspective: What a Good Boss Needs to Know

1. It is hard to be different from the majority, and it can bring an unwelcome spotlight. She is doing extra work to minimize the differences.
2. She is not always comfortable speaking up when people say offensive things; she doesn't want to mark herself as a problem.
3. She feels marginalized when colleagues excuse a statement based on how the speaker intended it, rather than judging by how it actually makes her feel.
4. Small comments may seem harmless in isolation, but she's getting them from different angles and people over time. They add up.

Don't Just Help Employees to Optimize Within Bad Situations; Change the Dynamic

Back in my days of deals and corporate spending accounts, troubling situations popped up frequently, and it's staggering to think back about how many stories my female colleagues shared with me. Once, my friend Kristin, a fellow investment banker, shared a story about a time she was flying on a private jet with a client CEO and his executive team—seven people in total, including her and her boss. She was the youngest person on the plane, but she was not the only woman. This executive team had two women in the C-suite, both of whom were on the flight, along with three male executives including the CEO. It was a gender-balanced environment.

On the jet, there were four seats in the front, two facing front and the other two across from those, facing backward. She had been told before boarding that the CEO always sat in what they called the "power seat," which was the forward-facing aisle seat in that cluster of four. Everyone else, she learned, would look to him to determine who he wanted sitting in the other three seats surrounding him. This was a good way to read who was most in favor with him at any given moment. If you weren't asked to sit in one of those seats, you went to the back.

Once in flight, the CEO was having an energetic conversation with Nancy, one of the female executives up front, and he called to the back of the plane. "Kristin! Come up here; you need to learn from this too." She unbuckled her seat belt and scurried up to the front, perching on the arm of Nancy's seat, prepared to listen eagerly.

The CEO continued addressing Nancy. "So, now that I've given you responsibility for the publishing unit, your first move needs to be to fire the existing head."

"Why?" protested Nancy. "She seems great."

The CEO patiently nodded and said, "This is the lesson. You're a thin, attractive woman. You are too, Kristin—that's why I wanted you to hear this." He paused for effect. "Thin, attractive women can't take the risk of having fat women work for them. They will resent you and undermine you." This advice struck Kristin as so offensive, and so impossibly wrong, that she thought he must be joking. She looked to Nancy for a cue as to how to react.

"She was nodding thoughtfully," Kristin recalled, "so I did too. She didn't say anything else or question his logic at all. She seemed to be making note of the advice in her head, and that was it. Then she thanked him for the advice and promised to remember it. So I thanked him too."

After the flight, Kristin asked Nancy privately about it, tentatively dancing around the fact that she thought the conversation was wildly inappropriate. Nancy advised Kristin that while she agreed it was inappropriate, she has found when their CEO feels strongly about something it's best to just go along with it.

"I asked if she was actually going to fire the woman he was talking about," said Kristin, "and she said, 'What? No! I will figure out a way to move her to another job in the company that's just as good.'"

Years later, I reflect on Kristin's story and feel that the executive team she was traveling with missed an opportunity to band together to change the dynamic. It was clear from their reactions that they had encountered this type of situation with their CEO before. Yet no one felt like they could challenge him. It can certainly be difficult to put yourself in the position of standing up to someone with more power than you. But there's safety in numbers. And it shouldn't have been handed down to others like Kristin to experience and tolerate that behavior. If you're in any situation like this, discuss it with your peers and find a way to challenge the behavior as a group. You have to take responsibility to stop that kind of toxic behavior from reaching people who have even less power than you do.

Take Full Responsibility for Protecting Employees from a Bad Situation

My own experiences mirrored those of Kristin and the other women we worked with. Again and again, when we looked for guidance on how to handle uncomfortable, gender-fueled conversations at work, the advice that we received was to just go with it—don't protest or disagree. The socially acceptable tactic seemed to be to do your best within the flawed structure of the workplace, without actually doing anything to change it. Work quietly in the background to protect others and avoid letting anyone get hurt, while not confronting the situation directly. It is easier to avoid direct confrontation, and as a middle manager it is risky to speak up. I never saw anyone speak up or protest these kinds of incidents. I took these examples to heart, and when I became a manager myself, I modeled my behavior after the managers who had guided me through these situations.

As we now know thanks to the #MeToo movement, pretty much every woman has encountered uncomfortable situations in the workplace where she, or someone she was close to, experienced some form of an unwelcome sexual advance. Because I had been so conditioned not to speak up against men in roles of authority in the workplace, I'm guilty of reinforcing this behavior as well. I once knowingly sent a young woman who worked for me into an inappropriate situation with a man that we worked with. Looking back now, I can't believe that I thought I was doing the right thing as her manager.

Here's what happened. Not long after this young woman joined the firm, a man, who was senior to both of us, started coming by our section of the office to chat with her frequently. One day around five o'clock, he asked her to go out for a drink with him. He said he wanted to talk about future opportunities for her. He told her to pick the bar and to be ready to go in thirty minutes. She came to me asking what to do.

In hindsight, I very obviously should have just said, "Don't go." Instead, I gave her what I now realize was terrible guidance. I jumped into action, calling upon my own experience in managing situations with men in nonconfrontational, agreeable ways. To me, the goal was always to keep it friendly. Never let a man feel like he was being rejected, but avoid a situation where anything bad could actually happen. I was still thinking like a dutiful employee instead of like a manager. So my solution was for her to go but control what we could about the situation. He said to pick the bar, so that's what we had control over. I set to work with another trusted colleague in strategically selecting the bar. We figured we could pick a well-lit, large, crowded bar, one that wouldn't provide an intimate setting, and she'd be fine.

She said she was nervous but she felt like she should go, and I told her I would stand by on my phone. Through the next two hours, I stayed in the office pacing. When she sent a quick email saying that he rejected her bar choice and insisted they go somewhere more "interesting," I started to panic. I kept checking in with her. She told me he kept steering the conversation back to sexual topics, no matter how hard she tried to change the subject. I told her she should make up an excuse and leave. She didn't feel like she could. I asked if she wanted me to come meet her there. She said she could handle it. More time passed, and then she finally called to say that she was home. I breathed a sigh of relief.

The next morning, she came in and gave notice of her resignation.

Although I was devastated by the experience, I had thought that it was at least a partial success because nothing physical happened. But, of course, something awful did happen: she was harassed and made to feel so anxious in the workplace that she did not want to return. At the time, I thought that he was the only bad actor because he had taken advantage of his seniority, and he had made her uncomfortable. But with management perspective, I have come to realize that while it's true that his actions were out of line, I played a role in this too. I knew nothing good was going to happen to her if she went out for drinks with him. I knew she didn't want to go, and instead of telling her not to, I added to the pressure by telling her that she should go and handle it the best she could. I was her manager and mentor, and it was within my power as her boss to intervene.

The problem was that I was only helping her to optimize within a bad system, rather than doing what I could to change the dynamic for her. The same was true of the staffer who encouraged me not to complain when I went to him about my discomfort working with Nathan. He advised me not to make a big deal out of it. And it was true of Nancy when she advised Kristin to smile and say thank you when given appallingly sexist lessons from her client. She advised Kristin to handle it quietly, rather than vocally object. These secondary characters in the stories were well intentioned and trying to be helpful by showing the smoothest, least controversial path forward. But they were more than innocent bystanders; they had the opportunity to change or stop the behavior, yet they didn't take responsibility. A good boss would have changed them instead of encouraging women to mold themselves to the circumstances, and that's what I should have done as well.

Changing the System Requires Managers to Speak Up (Which Isn't Easy)

Speaking up about inequity is important, but it isn't easy. A recent survey by global HR consultancy Randstad found that more than half of US employees know a woman who has been harassed at work, yet half of US employees also admit they've never spoken up when they hear a colleague make an inappropriate comment.[1]

"I worked for a guy for over seven years who was terrible to the women on our team. When I reflect on my own actions, the truth is I did very little about it," admitted one financial professional. "When you're a middle manager, things are stacked against you, and you have to protect yourself. The biggest impediment to speaking up was a real fear of losing my job. After the 2008 financial crisis, I was terrified to get fired. There were rampant layoffs—it felt like the world was ending. I didn't want to stand out in any negative way. On top of that, I didn't know if I could trust the HR function. I would talk about it with my peers—are they going to help you? Can you really have an honest discussion? Most of those HR relationships are stronger at the senior level, so how did I know that I could go to someone in HR and not have it come back to bite me?"

These honest and real fears for middle managers speak to the need for true structural changes in companies to create an environment where managers can push back and advocate for the women on their teams. When there is fear of retribution, it's unrealistic to tell every manager to just step up and do the right thing. Doing the right thing needs to be consequence-free. This is why anonymous HR hotlines continue to be valued by employees. There should always be a way for people to speak up without being identified.

There is a power dynamic in every organization, and it's not equally easy to challenge authority at all levels. The more power you have, the easier it is to speak up. So, if you are in a position of power, it is imperative that you make a point to be thoughtful and attentive to the challenges of underrepresented groups, and that you use the power that you have to speak up when you see inequities. It costs you less to do so than it does a middle manager.

But what if you aren't at the top of your organization? What are strategies that the average manager can use to speak up while not creating risk for themselves? Here are five ideas for speaking up, whether in the moment or after the fact.

Speaking Up in the Moment: Comfortable Honesty Through Humor

Humor is a great tool. Use it to deliver a message honestly while defusing the awkwardness that often comes with calling out a truth. It's a lighter-touch solution, so it tends to work with less significant moments, but every small battle that you can fight on behalf of someone on your team is worth fighting.

I was once asked to stand in for a male colleague at the last minute as a panel moderator at an education industry conference. The day of the conference, I spotted him and went over to say hello. He was chatting with one of the CEOs who would be on the panel, so he introduced me, saying that I was saving him by jumping in to replace him.

"Well," said the CEO he introduced me to, "this panel just got significantly better looking." It was a small thing, but it bothered me. Not only did I not want this random guy's opinion on my looks, but I wanted to be recognized as a benefit to the panel for substantive reasons: my experience, my perspective, my ideas. Sure, it could have just been a clumsy attempt to make fun of our mutual friend, the original panel moderator. That doesn't make it OK for some guy I just met in a professional setting to comment on my attractiveness.

In this case, our mutual friend jumped right in with a simple, "Don't say that, dude." That was all it took. Nothing dramatic, and nobody dwelled on it. He simply made the point and I appreciated it.

The trusty "Don't let HR hear that" category of jokes works quite effectively as well. "Whenever someone said something in my office that had an inappropriate tinge to it, we would all just yell, 'HR!'" recalled a midlevel manager. "It was funny, but you know, we also meant it."

Speaking Up in the Moment: Get Credit for Being Discreet

Company holiday parties are classic breeding grounds for bad behavior. A female manager told a story of an uncomfortable situation at her company's annual party. "A very senior leader was being really inappropriate with a young junior woman. Alcohol was involved. He was dancing really close, hanging on her. Somebody even said he licked her face.

"Everyone was watching it happen. Another woman on my team came to me and said, 'You have to do something.' She was right. Back then I remember feeling that when behavior like that crossed a line, there was less comfort confronting it. Especially at a party. I didn't want to make a scene. I was just as worried about upsetting him or embarrassing him as I was about how the young woman was feeling. That isn't fair, but that's what we learned and how we got along.

"I didn't call him out or embarrass him. I quietly steered him away, helped him leave the party, and got him out of there." This manager alleviated the situation within the existing construct. She intervened but didn't rock the boat. She did what she could. All managers can strive for more, but if you can do a little, it's better than doing nothing.

Speaking Up After the Fact: Recruit Someone with More Power Than You

When you don't feel you can say something yourself, think about the people with more power than you who you think would be able to speak when you can't. There's often someone on a senior team who is the right combination of being sensitive to the issue at hand and comfortable being direct about it. Ask them for help.

Being comfortable telling a senior executive to his face that you have a problem with what he did or said is a very high bar. Speaking up to a senior executive peer of that individual is way easier. Nobody said you always have to do things the hardest way possible; make use of this alternative path whenever you can.

Speaking Up After the Fact: Find Safety in Numbers

When a senior executive is the bad behaver in the organization, it often helps to talk about it with colleagues of equal status to you. You might not be comfortable speaking up directly to the senior executive, and you might not trust HR, but you can talk about it with other managers at your level and work through the possibilities for taking action.

"My natural inclination is to solicit advice from peers," shares one manager who grappled with the behavior of a senior executive in a large, multilayer organization. "As a group we would see things he did, and a few managers would get together and say, 'What do we do about it?'" When you do things as a group, responsibility gets diffused and the risk of retribution is lower. Talking about issues with others also creates accountability; once you've all acknowledged out loud that a problem exists, it gets harder to justify inaction.

Speaking Up After the Fact: Talk to Her About It

When you don't feel like you're in a position to confront the offender directly, there's still an important conversation you can have. It's with the woman who was impacted. Acknowledge that something happened, and apologize on behalf of the company. When you're a manager, you don't just speak for yourself; you speak for the organization that your employees are working within. When the organization fails her, you should be sorry, and you should tell her that.

One manager shared that he worries about speaking up in the moment. Not because of the risk to him and his career, but because he doesn't know how she feels about it. "What if she doesn't want to be defended, what if it makes her more uncomfortable, what if she just wants to drop it?" he speculates. "I don't know if calling attention to it makes her seem less strong, or like the damsel in distress. Then you've got some guy mad at you for stepping in, and she might be mad at you, too, for making an issue of it. There's a lot to lose, so it's very tempting to just pretend like nothing happened."

It may be true that she doesn't want the added attention that would come from making an issue of it in the moment. But after the fact, privately, you have more to gain by raising it to her and hearing what she has to say. If you ignore it, you run the risk that she feels unacknowledged, out of place in her work environment, and out of sync with you, her manager.

When you do bring it up to her, watch out for one more pitfall. It's human nature to get caught up in justifying and rationalizing. Don't focus on explaining why it wasn't your fault, how you would never have said that yourself, or how you think someone else should have done something about it. It's not going to make her feel better to know that you don't feel you're at fault. That only makes you feel better, so say that to yourself. To her, you need to own the situation, and genuinely express remorse for the impact it had on her. She'll respect you so much more if you do that, and she will feel much more respected and heard within the company.

The Consequence of Not Speaking Up

When I talk about speaking up, I don't mean only when you see something happening to someone with less power in the organization. It also means speaking up if something happens to you, or if you are aware of it happening to someone else. As many executives have come to terms with the #MeToo movement, they have recognized failings from the past when they kept quiet about things that happened. One woman told about hearing that a younger female colleague had filed a complaint with human resources when a senior executive made an inappropriate late-night phone call to her. Upon hearing the rumor, she went to the head of the human resources department and said, "I heard that this accusation was made, and I know it's true. I know it's true because he did the same thing to me."

A lot of women managers are looking back and questioning whether they let down younger women by not speaking up about things that happened to them. At the time, it seemed better not to say anything. They didn't want to embarrass themselves, but they also didn't want to embarrass the person who did it, or force anyone in the company to have to talk about an uncomfortable situation. There's a lesson in here for male managers too. When things happen, people talk about them. Women confide in others, and gossip spreads. If someone in the office is a repeat offender, you can usually bet that plenty of people in the office know about it.

Some companies have implemented "see something, say something" policies meant to create an explicit responsibility to report inappropriate behavior when you see, or hear, about it. So, if someone confides in you, or you hear about something happening to a colleague, you should report it. You might question whether it's really your place, or whether it's right to speak up when you don't know all the details or didn't hear about it firsthand. Knowing that offenders left unchecked tend to repeat themselves, you should report anything you hear about, anonymously if you're more comfortable doing it that way. It's the best way to protect possible future victims.

Pay Attention to the Little Things

These stories, and many like them, require a serious intervention to help extract a woman from an uncomfortable situation. But many other, less weighty, moments occur nearly every day, creating opportunities for a boss to address what is said and done around the office. A successful woman will pick her battles in an effort not to spend her chips on the little things, or to create a perception that she's difficult. But little things add up. As her boss, you can take on some of those battles so that she doesn't have to always be the one to speak up.

Keep an eye out for small offending comments. Many of them are about her appearance or demeanor. Comments on her outfit, her hair, her height. Whether or not she smiles enough. How young she looks. What her voice sounds like. These types of comments happen regularly. In isolation they are reasonably harmless, but compounded over time they really wear people down.

Making a rigid rule like "Don't ever comment on a woman's appearance" is oversimplifying. It's an abdication of responsibility when you try to reduce nuanced interactions to simple rules. Some people try to shortcut it by declaring, "I just won't have lunch or one-on-one meetings with women; it's the only way to steer clear of risk." It takes more active thought to gauge whether something is appropriate to say. A good rule of thumb is to ask whether the comment is about the employee's work or is about the employee as a person. Stay focused on the substance of her work.

But even that rule isn't hard and fast. You spend a lot of time with the people you work with, and you get to know some of them very well. In some cases, it's perfectly fine to comment on something personal. The better you know someone, the more likely it is that she will welcome your interest or your compliment. Just as you gauge your personal relationships and make different judgments about what is appropriate to say, you will have varying degrees of comfort with the people you work with. I had a business lunch recently with three of my board members: two men and one woman. We all know each other well. I walked in wearing a pink dress. "You look summery!" exclaimed one of the board members. "Oh wait," he interrupted himself. "I shouldn't have said that, right? Someone told me the other day that I shouldn't comment on women's outfits."

"It's fine," I said. "You only shouldn't comment on women's outfits if you're going to say something inappropriate. It's nice to give a compliment; it's not nice to make me feel uncomfortable by commenting on the way a dress looks on me or something like that. In this case, I appreciate the compliment!" And it's true—I did.

There are degrees of appropriateness, but I refuse to believe that we should retreat to a world where no one says anything nice or personal to anyone else. Giving a compliment, even one about someone's physical appearance, is welcome when it is positive, nonsexual, and said at an appropriate level of familiarity. This is where judgment comes in, and having good judgment is essential to being a good manager.

Good Boss Checklist: What You Can Do to Be a Better Boss for Women

1. Pay attention. Listen to what people are saying, be aware of their impact, and tailor your action to the situation.
2. Respond in the moment when it feels right, using humor where appropriate to create a comfortable learning opportunity not only for the offender but for the other witnesses.
3. Take the offender aside when the situation requires more conversation, explaining the impact of what they said and asking them not to do it again.

4. Jump in immediately when a situation is very uncomfortable or leading to a dangerous place, to put a clear stop to it and remove her from the situation.
5. Model good behavior. Give feedback and comments that are focused on the work, not the person.

THE CEO PERSPECTIVE: BIG IDEAS FOR COMPANY-WIDE IMPACT

Rosetta Stone: Board Representation

Being purposeful in filling management and executive roles with women is not only good for the sake of diversity; it's good for the bottom line. There are multiple benefits to having meaningful female representation in senior levels of an organization. A 2014 Gallup study found that businesses with more gender diversity produce "better financial outcomes than those dominated by one gender."[2] This is in large part due to the ability of a diverse organization to attract the best talent from the largest pool. Having some diversity brings more diversity. A 2019 *Harvard Business Review* survey found that "the most talented individuals go to places that do better with diversity, and this may be what is driving diverse firms in certain contexts to outperform their peers."[3]

Diversity of perspectives leads to more thoughtful decisions. Representation of all customer/client perspectives leads to better product-market fit. And, when those who work for and within the company feel that they can relate to their management team, it supports the development and promotion of more diverse talent at all levels of the organization.

There has been significant progress made toward increasing the representation of women on boards. There is a strong business case for having diversity at the board level, and the dialogue has moved beyond simply calling to have at least one woman on every corporate board, to calling for meaningful representation by women. Some studies have asserted that having a board's composition be at least

20 percent female is important.[4] Other measures focus on the absolute number of women needed on a board to have an impact. In 2007, Catalyst reported that when companies have three or more women on their boards, they perform better than average on financial metrics, including return on equity, return on sales, and return on invested capital.[5]

A 2006 report by the Corporate Executive Board found that having three or more women on a board was a critical tipping point for achieving positive impact: "While a lone woman can and often does make substantial contributions, and two women are generally more powerful than one, increasing the number of women to three or more enhances the likelihood that women's voices and ideas are heard and that boardroom dynamics change substantially."[6]

The report goes on to say that having women on a board creates value in three distinctive ways:

1. Women expand the range of discussion at the board level by taking into account a broader group of stakeholders, including shareholders, employees, customers, and the community.
2. Women ask challenging questions and are more diligent in pursuing answers.
3. Women bring a more collaborative approach to leadership and communication among directors and between the board and management.

In the early 2010s, there were more Fortune 1000 companies with no women on their boards than there were with three or more women.[7] This has changed significantly in recent years. With more vocal advocacy as well as legal mandates in some states, women's board representation has improved. In 2016, the average number of women on Fortune 1000 boards was up to 1.9.[8]

Like many education companies, Rosetta Stone, the language learning and literacy company, counts more women than men among its employees. The company has more than one thousand employees, and more than half are women. So the company set out to build a board of directors that is representative of the gender diversity of the employee and customer bases.

"At Rosetta Stone, with more than half of our employees, customers, and learners being female, having significant leadership from women on our board is not only appropriate, it's necessary," shares CEO John Hass. "The dialogue at the board level is more valuable when the voices in the room are representative of the people we serve. It's critical as we look to deliver positive solutions for learners and compete for, nurture, and retain talent in a tight job market."

Having deep female representation on boards requires deliberate goal setting and proactive recruitment. With the recent rush to source female board candidates, companies need to be thinking not only about what they stand to gain from board diversity, but also about how they can attract talented women to consider joining them. In California, for example, all public companies are now legally required to have at least one woman on the board, with additional requirements for larger boards. In this environment, women are going to increasingly have choices when considering which boards to join.

"Fortunately, because our work drives positive change in society, we have been able to attract world-class people to our board, including three women who bring deep experience in education, marketing and communications, culture, and leadership," says Hass. As one of those women, I can add that what is attractive about joining boards like Rosetta Stone's is that all board members prioritize active, balanced dialogue where every voice is given weight and value. Having multiple women on a board, rather than being the lone female voice, adds to the ability to participate and be heard in that active dialogue.

The Big Idea

Have three or more women on the board of directors.

Why It Works

- Broadens representation of the key stakeholders of the company.
- Gives weight to female voices.
- Enhances board communications among directors and with company management.
- Sends a top-down message of the importance of gender representation.

DON'T MAKE
HER ASK TWICE

A CFO once told me that he had a very simple cost control strategy: he never responded to a person's first request. As a working rule, he did not approve any requests to spend company money unless the person seeking the approval came back and asked him a second time. If they sent the first request by email, he never responded. If they asked him in person, he told them he'd think about it and get back to them, but never did. "If they come back and ask again, I know they really think it's important," he said. I filed that knowledge away.

Fast-forward a few years. I wanted to ask for more compensation. My job had always involved making acquisitions and investments, but lately I had been spending more of my time selling businesses that no longer fit within our company's mission. These sales generated tens of millions of dollars. We gave generous bonus packages to the executives who ran each business that we were selling, which they collected upon a successful sale. Despite the fact that no one had greater influence on whether we had a successful sale outcome than I did, I didn't get to participate in these bonus packages. Moreover, typically a company would hire an investment bank to run these types of deals, but because I had banking experience, I ran the deals myself, saving us millions of dollars in banker fees. So, I started thinking, *Bankers get paid a cut of the deals that they successfully complete. I should too.*

I had worked up the courage to propose a new bonus plan to my boss that was based on paying me a small percentage of each sale that I completed on behalf of the company. He seemed receptive, said he'd think it over and get back to me. He never did. At first I thought, *It takes time to work these things through HR—I shouldn't be pushy.* After more than two weeks went by and he said nothing, I thought, *Maybe this is one of those times that I'm supposed to ask twice.*

So I worked up even more courage and asked again, tentatively saying, "I wanted to follow up on the bonus proposal."

He looked at me blankly and for a second I thought, *Oh my god, he doesn't even remember.*

But then he said, "Oh sure, I'm working on it, but I don't have an answer for you."

I tried to clarify. "So, is it just a matter of timing to get it all set up, or does someone other than you need to approve it?"

He seemed irritated. He said, "Well, it was a pretty generous package you asked for, so I can't guarantee I can get you all of it. I have to see what I can do."

I still wasn't clear on who besides him would need to approve it, and whether he had even tried to do anything. He was a C-level executive, but he was talking as if the whole thing was out of his control. But I dropped it. I had the feeling that if I never brought it up again, neither would he. I was right; he never brought it up again. I gave up and started looking for another job. I assumed that, though he wasn't telling me no to my face, he didn't want to do it, so I should stop bothering him.

It's possible that what I needed to do was to keep asking my boss until it was easier for him to say yes than to continue putting me off. But the way I see it, my company lost a talented employee because of his lack of responsiveness to my request. The lesson for managers: if you want to retain your people, answer their questions. The first time. Give a clear, prompt, and honest response. Saying yes is best, but saying no is way better than giving no answer at all.

Men Are More Comfortable Asking Twice

After I became a CEO, I noticed that the men who reported to me on my executive team asked me for things all the time—more compensation, more responsibility, more budget. And then, when I said no, I noticed something else: the men would just ask me again. And again. Sometimes it reminded me of the impatient child who won't take no for an answer.

"Can I have some ice cream?"

"Not now, maybe later."

"How about now?"

"No, not now."

"Now?"

"No!"

And so on.

The women on my team asked me for things far less frequently. If I said no once, they rarely asked a second time. It struck me then that the CFO's rule of making everyone ask twice wouldn't work very well for women.

When Women Negotiate, It Backfires

The solution, unfortunately, is not simply to tell women to ask twice. People don't like it when women are pushy and ask for things more than once. They get exasperated, thinking, "I already told you no," or "I told you I'd get back to you." So women have learned over time that it's generally best not to push.

Glassdoor's 2017 Salary Negotiation Insights Survey revealed that only three in ten women negotiate their job offers, versus half of all men. But when they do negotiate offers, men are more than three times more successful than women in securing higher pay.[1] Many women have learned that asking for more is not a successful strategy for them.

I was on the board of a startup where I had a front-row seat as the COO, Sean, negotiated to hire a new sales executive, Tom. In this negotiation, Tom first asked for a higher salary. When Sean said no, Tom simply asked again, and pushed until Sean finally agreed. At our board meeting, Sean described this negotiation with a tinge of sheepishness. He had made a lot of concessions to Tom. But Sean still recommended moving forward and closing the deal. He joked, "If he can do this good of a job negotiating with me, imagine what he'll be able to pull off with our clients!"

The board approved the higher offer. But the story did not end there. Next, Tom started introducing new terms that had not previously been on the table: company stock, a relocation allowance, schedule flexibility, and his own seat on the board. Exhausted from the back-and-forth, Sean came back to the board asking us what to do. I argued to cut Tom loose. I felt that the continued asking and pushing was a bit too shameless and that it signaled a level of self-interest that I didn't feel a small startup like ours could afford to indulge.

The rest of the guys on the board felt otherwise; while they agreed that it was getting to be too much, they also felt that we had come so far and were so close to an agreement with him that they wanted to close the deal. So Tom was hired with a compensation package that was much richer than it was when we had started the conversation.

I tried to learn from the experience; I made a note to myself to embrace a little shamelessness in negotiation by asking beyond my comfort zone. After all, as the saying goes, "If you don't ask, the answer is no." There didn't seem to be any penalty for asking: Tom had asked for tons of stuff and in the end he got most of it, and no one seemed to hold it against him. Based on Tom's success, I started to suspect that men were not only asking more often, and for more than women were, but they were doing it unapologetically. They even seemed to be respected for it.

A few months later, this same company approached me to negotiate a buyout of my company's piece of the business. They offered us a good price, and I knew that I could simply take the deal and my boss would be happy with the result. But I remembered Tom's negotiation, and how much more money and respect this board had given him when he asked for more. I remembered my note to self to "embrace shamelessness" and decided to ask for more. I figured this would be a good test run for me, since I wasn't even asking for myself, but on behalf of my company. No one could accuse me of personal greed; I was just trying to be a responsible employee and get the best result for my company. This would be a neutral, less personal conversation.

I said I would agree to their proposed price, but that I wanted them to sweeten the pot with a small number of equity options. This would give the company back what they wanted (the shares and the voting control), while allowing my employer a small amount of continuing ownership, which I believed would become valuable as the company grew. It felt like a small, reasonable ask, and a respectful message overall: I was asking for options because I still believed in the company and its future. Much to my surprise, Sean balked at my proposal. He stammered and struggled to find words, finally spitting out, "I can't believe you would have the nerve to ask for this." I could picture his red face trembling with anger through the phone line. In fact, he was so deeply offended by my request that when I tried to explain it, he abruptly ended our conversation by hanging up on me.

I was confused by what had happened. I was willing to do what the company wanted and had only asked for one small extra thing. What had I done wrong? Then Tom, the very same executive who had aggressively negotiated his own compensation package, reached out to me. He advised me to go back and apologize to Sean, and to accept his original offer quickly, before he took it off the table. "You know," Tom advised me benevolently, "you don't want to be greedy about these things."

I revised my note to myself: being shameless works for some people, but not for everyone. Unfortunately, in my experience and that of most of the women I've spoken with, women are generally stuck in the group for whom it doesn't work very well.

Many other women have tried versions of what I attempted. They watch a similarly situated man pull off a successful negotiation, or they get advice from a trusted male advisor to try negotiation tactics that worked for him. But when these women attempt to put those same strategies to work for themselves, it backfires.

In a striking number of cases, women have told me stories of managers, male and female alike, who not only don't like or respect women's attempts to negotiate, but they simply refuse to engage in the negotiation conversation at all, hanging up phone calls and pulling deals and offers in reaction to even the smallest requests.

> For specific advice for women on how to successfully navigate around these pitfalls, see the box "Advice for Women: Five Tips for Negotiating a Job Offer in Today's Imperfect System" in the appendix.

When Emily, a twenty-eight-year-old finance professional, was seeking a job upon graduation from her MBA program at Stanford, she lost out when she attempted to negotiate a job offer. She had been talking to a company for a while and was very excited about the opportunity. When they made the formal offer, she was surprised that it was for less salary than she had expected based on previous conversations with the CEO. "I had gotten advice from a few different guys in my business school class that everyone negotiates an offer, and in fact it's viewed as weak to not ask for more. So I thought asking for a higher salary was a normal thing to do and figured the worst that could happen is they'd say no."

But when Emily asked for more salary, the CEO of the company promptly rescinded the offer, with no further discussion or explanation. Emily went on to work at another company, but the experience continues to bothers her. "It still sticks with me," Emily told me. "I wonder what I could have done differently. I know that men negotiate offers all the time, so I'm not sure why it didn't work for me."

I happen to know the CEO who rescinded Emily's offer, so I asked him about it. He certainly felt badly about it, but also felt confident that he had made the right call in pulling her offer. "I didn't want to be in a position where I brought in someone who wasn't 100 percent excited to be there, or was a flight risk from the start because she was getting less money than what she really wanted," he recalled.

The problem with this perspective is that the CEO was ascribing feelings and desires to this woman based on his own beliefs rather than based on the facts of the negotiation. He didn't actually know how excited she was about the potential job, and he didn't know how his inability to agree to her higher salary request would impact her excitement, if at all. He could have told her that he couldn't meet her salary demand and let her decide whether she still wanted the job on those terms.

When managers bring their own baggage about women to the negotiation, they are loading the conversation with unstated assumptions that a woman can't possibly respond to. Research finds that men in particular penalize women for *initiating* negotiations, regardless of what was actually said or done in the negotiation itself. The mere expectation of a negotiation triggered men to express beliefs about the "niceness" versus the "demandingness" of the women, in a way that they did not do with other men.[2] It's burdensome for women to have to worry not only about what they say, but also about what someone might think they are thinking when they say it.

In Emily's case, she might have made an informed decision to accept a lower offer and be happy with it even when it was for less than she requested. Or she could have just said no. But the CEO did not give her the chance to decide for herself. He decided for her that if he didn't give her the full salary she asked for in negotiation, she would never really be happy in the job.

Melissa, a thirty-nine-year-old executive, was offered a VP operations role at a company that she was excited about. But the offer was lower than her current salary, plus she already had a C-level title in her current company. So she thanked the CEO for the offer but asked if it would be possible to match her current title and salary. "The CEO told me that he was 'disappointed' that I would ask," said Melissa. "I guess I was supposed to just want the job that he offered, and not ask for anything more."

Another woman, an MBA graduate from the United States who was working in London, was recruited by a leading Silicon Valley technology firm. Her discussions with them culminated in an offer. She was excited about the job and happy with the pay, so she accepted the offer and gave notice to her London employer. In her follow-up discussions with the tech firm, she asked them to clarify who she would be reporting to and requested more details about her future role and responsibilities. Instead of answering her questions, the firm rescinded their offer.

They told her that she wasn't a culture fit after all. People at the company didn't get "hung up" on things like reporting lines. At this point she had resigned from her job in London, which ended her work visa and started the clock ticking on the time she was legally allowed to remain in the United Kingdom. The tech firm was supposed to be arranging for her relocation back to the United States. She tried to reach out to discuss and bring them back to the table, but the damage was done and they would not engage with her further. Left stranded and scrambling, she paid the ultimate price for asking questions.

With stories like these getting passed around, it is no surprise that many women are reluctant to ask for anything at all. Women put tremendous time and energy into thinking about what to ask for, and how to ask it, to minimize the chance that they come across as too aggressive or difficult. On the flip side, they worry that if they don't ask, they will be perceived as weak or unimpressive. The result is that women have to devote time to preparing, practicing, and moderating their negotiation requests before they make them, time that many men never have to spend. The negotiating tactics that work for men just don't work for women.

Understanding Her Perspective: What a Good Boss Needs to Know

1. She is hesitant to negotiate because it has backfired before.
2. She wants to maximize her pay, just like men do.
3. She doesn't want to seem pushy, but she also doesn't want to seem like a pushover.
4. It was hard enough for her to ask the first time, so she probably won't ask a second time.

It Doesn't Work for Women to Just Negotiate Like Men Do

I once was on a panel with other female investors, gathered to give advice to young female entrepreneurs about how to go about fundraising for their startups. I listened to a partner from a prominent venture capital fund give the audience what I consider to be incomplete advice. "I always tell female founders this," she said. "In the time that it took you to draft and edit your pitch email to me, I received a hundred less well-written emails from men, and I already picked one of them to fund." The implication was clear: get out of your heads, stop spending so much time thinking about how to ask for things, and just ask.

The investor was telling women all of this is easier for men, so you should act more like men and then it will be easier for you too. But it doesn't work when women try to do what men do. There is a reason that women spend all that time and emotional energy thinking about how to ask for something. When we don't go out of our way to soften every request and position ourselves just perfectly, we tend to get rejected. So we have adapted ourselves to the male-dominated world we live in in a way that maximizes our results.

In all negotiations, people bring the context of their past interactions and experiences with them. To negotiate well, you need to be able to see the perspective of the other and anticipate what matters most to them. So it's only natural that managers are calling upon their own context when negotiating with their employees. The challenge for women is that, because it is more common for men to negotiate, the context men bring to their negotiations with other men is likely much deeper and more diverse than the context they have for women at work.

Recognize the Extra Work That Women Do to Make Their Negotiation Acceptable

I still catch myself going down a rabbit hole of self-editing and self-doubt when negotiating for pay. A few years ago, I agreed to do some expert consulting for an investment firm, and they sent me their standard consulting agreement with a rate filled in that was less than half of the hourly rate I was billing for similar clients.

I opened a reply window and started to write: "That's less than half my normal rate—I would need to charge you $x per hour." I imagine that many men would have just written that and clicked *send*. But I knew I couldn't do that; it was too risky. Like most women, I paused and thought carefully about how to write an email that would best convey my confidence in my value, while not being too aggressive.

So I added another sentence at the beginning of my reply, to start the email out with a more positive tone: "Thanks for sending. The agreement looks pretty straightforward other than the rate . . ." (*"I'm a positive and agreeable person!"*)

I added some more context around the rate I had charged others. (*"Other smart men have already paid me this much."*)

Next, I noted that I knew this could lead to great future opportunities, so I wasn't focused on maximizing the rate, just on making it reasonable. (*"I'm not greedy."*)

I gave some options—we could increase my hourly rate, or agree upon a fixed cost for the full project. (*"I'm flexible."*)

Finally, I reread the email a few more times, wordsmithing here and there to make sure it sounded casual, flexible, and agreeable, while also being clear and confident.

In the end, I spent more than twenty minutes drafting, editing, reading, rereading, sitting on it, revisiting it, second-guessing it, revising it, and finally clicking *send*, followed by a panic that maybe I shouldn't have asked and now they were probably going to cancel the whole thing, and maybe I should have just taken their rate because some money is better than no money and I really did want to do the project.

About a minute after I sent my email, the partner at the investment firm responded: "No problem, we'll pay the rate you quoted." I got my desired outcome. To get there, I had to put in extra effort and time, which took away from other, more productive, things I could have done with that time. While we can't know for sure if I needed to do all of that versus simply asking like a man, I've found success when I go through all of these extra rounds of careful editing, and I have had little success when I don't. Many women feel the same. We have a nagging feeling in these situations that, with meaningfully less effort, a man would get not just an equivalent result, but possibly a better one.

One of the most important things this book is doing is shining light on that extra effort that comes from navigating a workplace that is not made for women. It's why we need more bosses that change the environment to be what works for women, instead of teaching women how to change themselves to fit the environment. Adapting to a work structure created by men, for men, takes a lot of extra work for women. The more we change that structure, the more meaning-ful the reduction in this emotional energy work will be.

The Best Solution: Offer Before She Has to Ask

When I first went to work for Mandy at Tutor.com, I didn't have to negotiate my job offer at all. As we discussed the role and the offer that she would make, the conversation further reinforced that she was going to be a different type of boss. I was expecting an offer that would be for more money overall than what I had been making at Kaplan, but in the form of a lower base salary paired with a higher bonus potential. Instead, she offered me both a higher salary and a bigger bonus plan. She said that she appreciated that I had been will-ing to take a lower base salary, but that she wanted me to feel valued from the start, and she knew I was worth the additional money.

I never had to negotiate because she did it for me. And she was right to do so. I was the best talent she could bring to her company for what she was trying to do. I was worth it. The work that I would do for her, and the added loyalty she generated by being fair and generous to me up front, would more than pay back the additional dollars spent on me. It was a smart management decision that generated a positive return for the company. It also meant that I spent less time agonizing over how to negotiate the offer and more time thinking about how excited I was to accept it.

Even if women do successfully ask for and receive a higher salary, they will feel less valued than if you had recognized their worth in your opening offer. So, instead of making women ask, make the offer proactively. If your supervisor or HR department gives you an offer range for a position but encourages you to start low to allow for negotiation, argue to go out with the high end and deliver it as a best and final offer. It saves you the hassle of a back-and-forth negotiation, and it removes the possibility that one person gets shortchanged simply because she didn't ask, or didn't ask in the right way.

There are costs to having inequities in your organization. Unless they are addressed, you will lose talented women who feel undervalued and seek a more rewarding environment elsewhere. Employees will spend time talking and thinking about the wage gaps and will be distracted and angry when they suspect or discover that a colleague is getting paid more. Women will devote time to working up the courage to ask for a salary adjustment and making sure that they ask in the right way. All of this is time that could instead be spent working productively for the company.

Good Boss Checklist: What You Can Do to Support Women at Work

1. Expect that women, like men, will advocate for themselves.

2. Give a clear answer when she asks for something, whether it's yes or no.

3. Never rescind an offer because someone negotiates. This doesn't mean that you should give everyone what they ask for, but it is not a reason to cut someone loose just because they asked.

4. Don't impose motivations into the heads of women when they are negotiating with you. Assume that if they accept your final offer, they are 100 percent on board.

5. Offer before women have to ask. Avoid the additional stress that comes with salary negotiations by making an offer that exceeds her expectations.

THE CEO PERSPECTIVE: BIG IDEAS FOR COMPANY-WIDE IMPACT

Match Group: Conduct a Third-Party Compensation Audit

Match Group, based in Dallas, Texas, is an online dating company that owns and operates some of the largest dating apps in the world, including Match.com, OkCupid, Hinge, and Tinder. With more than two thousand employees, 40 percent of whom are women, the company has made it a priority to ensure gender pay equity. A December 2018 external audit confirmed that the company had achieved 100 percent pay equity by gender, and the company continues to conduct annual audits to monitor and ensure that pay remains in balance.

The audit wasn't just conducted, presented, and put away in a confidential file. The company chose to publish its results, not only to all employees but in the press as well. Taking this approach shows that the company is holding itself to the results, not just making a symbolic gesture toward trying to be better. "Once you start it, you have to commit," shares Mandy Ginsberg, who was CEO of the company at the time the initial audit was conducted. "People know you're doing it and expect follow-up. I had watched Marc Benioff very publicly commit Salesforce to close any pay gaps, and ultimately end up spending over $10 million to do it. As a CEO of a publicly traded company, you have to be prepared for what it may take to make things right."

Achieving pay equity is about more than just keeping track of it. Ginsberg attributes Match Group's success to the approach they take to compensation from the very beginning of their employee relationships. Ginsberg and her human resources team hold themselves to a proactive compensation approach. Too often they saw employees, usually women, who would champion their teams but wouldn't advocate for raises for themselves. The Match team wanted to pay for performance rather than rewarding only those who ask. This philosophy applied to new hires as well. Instead of making offers based on what they think a candidate is likely to accept, or making offers that "leave room" for a candidate to negotiate, the Match HR department makes best offers out of the gate that are intended to reflect the entirety of what the employee is worth to the organization. They don't believe in leaving money on the table just because an employee doesn't ask for it.

"One of my guiding principles as a leader has always been rewarding employees based on their impact on the organization, whether they ask for it or not. I've never believed in pay structures where you only pay the squeaky wheels, or wait and pay people what they deserve only when they are threatening to walk out the door to a competitor."

The system was designed to be fair for everyone. The result was particularly beneficial to women. "So often and in so many businesses, women don't make compensation demands," Ginsberg shared. "And until we raise our daughters to make those demands, we, as leaders, need to be proactive and methodical about how we think about compensation."[3]

The Big Idea

Hire an outside firm to audit compensation to identify and correct gender inequity.

Why It Works

- Demonstrates to employees that you're not just
  giving lip service to pay equity.
- Uncovers any differences within the organization
  that may be driven by individual manager
  behavior.
- Moves the conversation about pay equity
  beyond goals and assumptions to tangible data.

BE AN EQUAL OPPORTUNITY ASSHOLE

headed into the office of the CEO one afternoon to present the financial model that I had been working on for a potential deal. I brought along my direct report, a younger woman who had built the financial model under my direction. We had spent hours preparing for the meeting. A lot of calculations used to value parts of a company are pretty straightforward, but we were trying to justify a dollar value for the brand reputation of the company we were buying, which is a pretty theoretical thing to try to put a number on. We had made some admittedly creative assumptions. He relentlessly grilled us, firing off question after question until he zeroed in on what he considered to be a flawed assumption.

"That's idiotic," he declared. "Why would you think that was a good idea?"

I tried to explain. "We needed a starting point and it felt reasonable to assume—"

He held up his hand to signal me to stop talking. He dramatically put his head in his hands. He took a deep breath.

"Go away," he barked. "This is garbage." To emphasize his point, he gathered the printed pages of the model output that we had brought to him and threw them in the general direction of the garbage can in his office. The papers scattered on the floor.

"OK," I said calmly. "I'll take that part out. I have another idea for how to do it."

"Fine, fine," he said with a wave of his hand. "Just bring me back something better."

We left his office, and I could see that my direct report was rattled.

"Why do you put up with working for him?" she asked me. "He's such an asshole."

"True," I responded, "but he's an equal opportunity asshole. He yells at me the same way he yells at the guys."

We reached the door of my office and I paused before going inside.

"And," I added, "he was right. That was a flawed approach we took in the model, but I think I know how to make it better."

Among the bosses I've had, some of them have been pretty volatile characters. Powerful, smart men with big egos who are widely said to be tough to deal with. I've never before or since been criticized as harshly as I was by each of them. And I don't think I would have advanced in my career without them. Each was incredibly smart and purely meritocratic in rewarding intelligence and competence in others. So, while they could be mean, they usually weren't wrong. And, most importantly, they were just as mean to me as they were to all the men in the room.

To be clear, I'm not urging managers to be cruel or to make their employees uncomfortable. (See Rule #2: Be Someone She Can Relate To, Rule #6: Speak Up So That She Doesn't Have To, and Rule #9: Tell Her That You See Her Potential.) But it's good for talented women to be held to high standards. Unlike many other managers, these "asshole bosses" aren't all that concerned about how you feel about your work. All they care about is what you can produce. If you have a good idea, they listen and reward it. If they need somebody to do something and they think a woman on their team is the most capable of doing it, they give it to her to do.

I took some of my biggest career leaps under the direction of this type of manager. After putting me through the wringer to prove my intelligence and worth, responsibility and opportunity followed, and it catapulted me in my career, ultimately all the way to the C-suite. When others watched me stand up under the scrutiny of difficult managers, I earned their respect too.

In one meeting, I had built the financial plan for a business unit and was helping that unit's leadership team present and defend their numbers to our CEO, another classic "equal opportunity asshole." I had prepared extensively, knowing that he wouldn't go easy on me. Sure enough, he pushed me aggressively, interrogating me on the depths of the financial model. After going several rounds, it became clear that he wasn't going to let up until he found something I couldn't answer. He kept asking more challenging questions, testing me to see how thoroughly I had prepared. Eventually, I tripped up and couldn't answer something. I don't even remember what it was. It was like playing a video game, where you make it to level 15, further than anybody else in the room could have made it, but you still didn't get to the giant banana at the end.

The CEO smiled and said, "You should have known that." I nodded. He was right—I should have known it. With no further questions, he approved the business unit's plan. He had proven his point. And that *was* the point. I believe he had decided to approve the plan long before he stopped asking questions. In the moment, I felt like he was just giving me a hard time. But he also gave me a very public forum to showcase how much I knew.

When debriefing afterward with my other colleagues who were in the meeting, they were all in awe of me. One of them said to me with admiration in his tone, "Wow, he really drilled you. He's come down hard on me before, but he just wasn't letting up on you no matter what. I'm bringing you with me every time I need to get something approved by him."

Make Sure Her Voice Is Heard

Beth is an executive who has run billion-dollar businesses with thousands of employees over the course of her career. Along the way, she worked for some equal opportunity assholes, and she believes it helped to develop her ability to advocate for her ideas. "Men tend to build respect confrontationally," she said. "It's not something that women do to each other." Guys in the office pick on each other, call each other out, and are openly competitive. When women are left out of that, it leaves them at a disadvantage.

"The willingness of a man to respect somebody enough to intellectually spar, to push on an idea . . . for a capable woman, it's gold. You get to show what you can really do." As a manager, if you tend to get competitive with the men who work with you directly, make sure you do the same with the women. You may think you're being respectful by not challenging her, but really it suggests that you don't respect her capabilities enough to think she can take it. Give her a chance to prove herself.

Doing it well, in Beth's experience, requires giving a woman a seat at the table, letting her actually get her own idea out, challenging that idea at the table just as men do to each other, and, perhaps most importantly, letting the woman answer. If a boss can do that for a woman, even if it's not done in the nicest way, it's valuable.

She recalled a time she experienced equal opportunity asshole treatment and was better off for it. She was the number two in command of her business unit and was asked to present her business performance to a group of the fifty top executives of the company, including the CEO and many of her peer leaders of other business units and divisions. In the middle of that presentation, she came to a slide in which she was making a point about her business that she felt strongly about. The CEO disagreed and challenged her point aggressively. He told her that he wanted her to pause the presentation, take a good look at the slide, and think about whether she was really making the right point. The entire room sat in silence and looked at her, looking at the slide, for three full minutes. "If you've never stood in front of a crowd in silence for three minutes, just know that three minutes is a long time," she noted. Her boss gave her the silence and let her figure it out for herself. He didn't try to fill it or use it to tell her what she should do. She stood there and thought it out, and then proceeded to make the case for her perspective. "I'll tell you what," she recalled. "I don't even remember what the point was that I made that day. But everyone remembers that meeting; people still bring it up to me. My reputation took a big leap forward that day."

I'm Not Crying, You're Crying . . .

The problem with equal opportunity assholes, of course, is that they're not always nice. In many of my conversations with women about times their bosses pushed them, they saw the value in it, but also conceded that it's hard. Ann, a publishing executive, emphasizes the nuanced reality that all managers have positives and negatives. "I had one boss who always told me exactly what I did wrong. But he also always told me how well I did. I came to really respect and enjoy working with him because I always knew where I stood. But sometimes I would go back to my office and cry. Now I look back and think: Honest was fantastic. Blunt and brutal, not OK."

It is good to challenge a woman, but there are degrees of kindness in the way it can be done. That said, if a woman does cry, it's not the worst thing in the world. "When someone cries in my office, inevitably they will apologize for it. I tell them there is no need to apologize—it simply shows how deeply they care and is a totally normal thing," says one manager. Worrying that you need to be careful about criticizing women because they might start crying can create unnecessary caution or avoidance of having honest conversations and giving feedback.

If you're going to be a good manager of women, you should probably figure out how to get comfortable with crying, because women have a higher biological propensity for tears. Women have 6 times as much prolactin (the hormone that generates tears) as men do, and are 4.5 times as likely to cry at work.[1] Forty-one percent of women report that they have cried in the workplace at some point in their careers. "Managers keep boxes of tissues on their desk for a reason," says Alison Green, author of the career advice blog *Ask a Manager*.[2]

Many women are emotionally invested in their work, and though they often go to great lengths to hold in their emotions, inevitably biology takes over sometimes. These moments are most likely happening behind closed doors. Crying in the ladies' room at work is a real thing; I've done it more than once, and I'm willing to bet that, off the record, you'd get far more than the 41 percent to admit in confidence that they've done it too. The important thing is to recognize that when someone cries at work, it is a biological reaction unrelated to their ability to perform the job. It's also an indication of how much they care about doing a good job, which is a good thing.

Knowing that a woman will feel embarrassed if and when she cries, you can help as a manager by minimizing her embarrassment. Focus on two things: 1) don't overreact if it does happen, and 2) minimize the chances that it happens in front of a large crowd. If you expect feedback to be difficult to take, save your criticisms for private meetings.

Part of being a supportive boss is acknowledging that emotions can run high at important moments, and if a woman needs to cry, give her the space and comfort to let it happen without a lot of fanfare. "I learned in an annual performance review that I would not be getting a promotion as had been previously implied," shared Amy, a marketing executive. "My manager and his boss were both there. As the news sank in, I was obviously upset and was trying really hard to hold it in. They definitely looked surprised when my face turned red. Then one of them actually commented about how my face was red, and that was it, Niagara Falls had started. I tried really hard to control it and continue with the conversation. They kept asking me if I was OK, which only made it worse."

It runs a little counter to a lot of the other advice about being direct and addressing things head-on, but when it comes to crying, it's actually best to only barely acknowledge it and just let it happen. Whatever you do, don't ask her if she's OK. It's so much harder to hold in the tears when somebody asks that question. And by all means *don't* tell her to calm down.

Once, I was out to dinner with a group of colleagues, nine of us seated around a large round table, cocktails served, waiting to order our meals. The CFO was in town and had invited a group of us out. He shared that he'd been at a dinner with friends over the weekend where someone had asked a great question, and everybody went around the table answering it. So he thought we'd do it here tonight. The question was "What's the worst thing your spouse ever said to you?"

In general, I wouldn't recommend this question at a work dinner. But we all knew each other well, so we rolled with it. A young paralegal, who was typically pretty reserved, jumped in without hesitation. "Oh, you won't believe what my husband said to me once," she declared. We were all intrigued. First, she gave the background. "He was late getting home from work, which meant that we would be late getting over to my parents' house for dinner, and I was all worked up about it." We all nodded in understanding; we'd all had versions of that argument with our partners. She continued, "But then he said one word to me, and he will never say it again."

We all speculated in our minds, and when we compared notes later, we found our thoughts had all been moving in the same direction. We figured it was a certain word our moms taught us never to say.

Everybody leaned in toward the center of the round table waiting for her to say the word. "He said . . . *relax.*"

The table collectively gasped.

"And I said," she continued, rising slightly out of her chair and jabbing her finger in the air, "Don't you tell me to relax. *You relax.*"

How true, we all agreed. "Relax" is absolutely the worst thing you can say to somebody when they are worked up about something. Crying is the same way. "Don't cry" or "Calm down" are not helpful things to say. Don't suggest in any way that crying is not the appropriate reaction to the situation. Just ask if she'd like to keep going, or if she'd like to take a break.

If she asks for a minute to regroup, you should leave the room, not the other way around. Don't make her walk out into a possibly public space and have others see that she was or is crying. That will only prolong the incident because she will then have to explain to well-meaning colleagues what has happened, they will ask her if she's OK, and the tears will start flowing again. Let her remain where she is, collect her thoughts, and then come back and proceed as if it didn't happen. And if, on the other hand, she says she wants to continue the conversation without a break, just keep going and don't revisit it by asking her if she's all right. The further into the conversation she gets, the more she'll be able to pull through the tears and move on.

Understanding Her Perspective: What a Good Boss Needs to Know

1. It's worse to feel that a boss is going easy on you than it is to be pushed by a difficult boss.
2. She appreciates being challenged, as long as she is also given the opportunity to speak in her own defense.
3. Women try really hard not to cry at work, and they are embarrassed when it happens.
4. Compliments mean more to her when they come from someone who also criticizes, because she knows it's honest.

Challenge Her, but Don't Put Her on the Spot

Challenging her work is valuable only when you also give her the opportunity to defend her ideas and demonstrate her abilities. In the workplace, these opportunities usually come in the form of the group meeting. A review of thousands of survey and feedback forms on the topic of meeting participation found that while men viewed women as "not loud enough" and felt they "allowed themselves to be interrupted," women felt that their greatest struggle with articulating their views was "due to timing." As a manager, think of yourself as a discussion moderator. It goes a long way to guide a conversation, to ask individuals to contribute and to elevate any ideas that are getting drowned out. Ensure equal opportunities to speak versus running your meetings as an open forum where everyone jumps in.[3]

In speaking competitions, there is a notable gender gap in performance in the Extemporaneous Speaking category. In these events, which require impromptu public speaking with "limited preparation," men perform significantly better than women: one study analyzed the results of national speaking competitions and found that out of a starting field that was 47 percent female, only 21 percent of the finalists were female. These performance gaps were greatly reduced in the Public Address event, where preparation time was allotted as part of the competition. In that competition, 46 percent of the finalists were women.[4]

We see equally striking gaps in the world of performance comedy. Women make up only 8 percent of headline performances at major comedy clubs.[5] Earning a spot on these stages typically requires a path through improvisational performance.

Put simply, women are generally not as comfortable winging it as men are. So putting her on the spot is not necessarily productive. I had one boss who would turn to me on the way into a board room and say, "Why don't you take section two of the slides?" Or worse, in the middle of the actual meeting, without warning, he'd say, "Kate, can you take this one?" My performance in those cases was not nearly as strong as with a different boss, who would tell me at least a day before a big meeting which parts he wanted me to be prepared to present. I needed time to organize my thoughts and map out what I wanted to say.

This doesn't mean that there's no value in learning how to think on your feet. But the office is not an improv stage, and you get to decide as a manager what kind of an environment you will foster. "You need to be sensitive to the individual style, to be productive in getting the most out of someone," shares Jonathan Grayer. "Early in my career, I didn't understand that not everyone had a high processing speed. I learned to give more time."

When I worked for Jonathan initially, he often asked me to contribute on the spot. But he didn't get the best out of me. Then, about a month before a big executive off-site, he asked me to research the international growth strategy of a competitor and prepare a presentation to the group focused on what that competitor was doing better than us. It was a dynamic, interactive group, so I could expect to be challenged in the meeting. But with a month to prepare, and a clear expectation of what I needed to do, I came in ready to impress in that meeting. It was a big turning point for me reputationally at the company because I was able to really show people what I could do.

Companies and teams benefit most from having diverse perspectives, so it's important not to push women into adapting to the male style of decision-making. It's OK that some people take their time in gathering and evaluating input before thinking or deciding. Learning where your direct reports sit on this spectrum and adapting to their styles will be much more successful than trying to force them to adapt to someone else's style.

A 2015 study of gender differences in managerial decision-making found differences, and different strengths, in the decision-making approach and effectiveness by gender. Men were found to make quicker, more linear decisions, which can be very effective in driving to an outcome. Women, on the other hand, were more successful in considering multidimensional factors and taking informal sources of information into account when making decisions.[6]

"Diversity of all kinds brings balance to decision making—ethnic, socioeconomic, and gender diversity all lead to better decision making," says Grayer.

Teach Her How to Defend Her Ideas

Another time in my early years at Kaplan, Jonathan decided to establish a new "numeracy" standard for our teams. Not everyone was equally comfortable defending their numbers and answering questions about financial data. In Jonathan's view, being numerate, able to understand and work with numbers, was as important as being literate in the traditional sense of being able to read and write. To accomplish this, he felt as a manager that he needed to provide resources and treat this as a training initiative. So a copy of Robert Anthony's *Essentials of Accounting* workbook showed up on everyone's desk a few days later, along with a deadline for completing the assignments in the workbook. All workbooks had to be turned back into Jonathan.

Because I had a degree in finance and accounting, I was exempted from the assignment. I will admit that I gloated about this; getting out of something that everyone else had to do was cause for delight. But what it meant was that I spent a lot of time helping others get through their workbooks. Most of the people that I helped were women. When I asked Jonathan about it years later, he shared, "It wasn't a program designed with gender in mind; it was something everybody needed. But when I reflect back, I do think it helped more women."

I've continued to implement that approach in my own companies. Offer training to ensure equal confidence in working with, interpreting, and talking about numbers. This doesn't have to be for women only, but my experience, similar to what we saw at Kaplan, is that financial training does tend to benefit women disproportionately, so it's a great resource to offer.

Sam, a CEO, also believes in using numbers as a fair way to challenge ideas while holding everyone to the same standards. "Data is a great equalizer and democratizer," he says. "So much influence in an organization is social or positional, and so much of that is gender biased. With data analysis, there's a basis to be equally tough on everyone." He cautions, however, that you need to make sure you educate your teams on how to use data to advocate for an idea. "Data can be interpreted and debated. People use and wield data in meetings differently." People who use data confidently have an edge over those who don't; they are often able to present their ideas as foregone conclusions if others don't know how to poke holes in their data. To create a fair environment, you need to teach everyone how to do that with confidence.

Honesty Is the Best Policy

What's great about "equal opportunity assholes" is their relentless honesty. They tell you how it is. You know exactly where you stand. You know what you need to do to be better. But the best ones also know when it's time to shift that honesty from focusing on what's wrong to highlighting what is positive. Compliments from these bosses take on outsized significance because they don't come easily, and because you know that they wouldn't say it if it weren't true.

In contrast, there are pitfalls in being too careful. It's counterproductive to be too nice. I worked for one manager who I could tell was nervous to give me direct feedback, as if he thought I would cry at the slightest bit of criticism. All my male peers referred to that banker as a tough guy to work for, one who always had a litany of criticisms for your work. With me, he hardly ever had a negative word to say. My colleagues told me I was either lucky or really good at my job. I don't think I was either of those things; I think he had just as many criticisms for me as for the others—he was just too uncomfortable to voice them to me. That made him a bad boss. He wasn't helping me improve. I didn't learn anything working for him. The idea that men must be chivalrous to women at work embraces outdated gender roles. Everyone should be respectful to all individuals at work, but respectful and careful are two different things.

Differences between perception and reality at work hold women back in very real ways. In most workplace relationships, the risk is high that a woman doesn't have an accurate read on how she is viewed. The more open, honest, and direct you are comfortable being with a female employee about the good and the bad in her performance, the more successful she can ultimately be.

According to a 2009 study presented by the Academy of Management, men and women perceive their own standing among colleagues differently.[7] Men do a better job overall of accurately estimating what a colleague thinks of them, whereas women underestimate how others see them. This is sometimes called a "confidence gap," although that can be a dangerous label here since we are not talking about women doubting their own abilities. What they are doubting is whether or not others see their capability. They don't see enough evidence that people think highly of them.

These differences are most pronounced when it comes to their bosses. Women are three times as likely as men to underrate their bosses' opinions of their job performance. Male workers tend to guess on the high side, believing that their bosses think slightly more highly of them than they actually do. Women, on the other hand, believe that their bosses think less of them than reality shows. Women don't know where they stand, so their best guess is good versus great even when their bosses in fact think quite highly of their performance.

"Women tend to always underestimate the esteem with which I hold them in our managerial relationship," shares Jake, a CEO. "It is so fun as a manager to get to give positive affirmation. I see that as my role for the talented female managers who work for me, to clearly say, 'You're great, go forward.'"

Another CEO reflected on a recent piece of feedback he received from one of the women who works for him. "She said, 'I feel like I'm on thin ice with you.' She felt like if she made one mistake she would be out. I had no idea she thought I saw her that way. I actually have so much confidence in her, and I'm extremely committed to having her here. It made me recognize that I needed to change the way that I give her feedback."

Because of this dynamic, it's particularly valuable as a boss of a woman to tell her explicitly when you are happy with her performance. Don't be so honest about her areas for improvement that you leave her worrying that you might not see all her capabilities, or that you might not think she's a top performer.

Good Boss Checklist: What You Can Do to Be a Better Boss for Women

1. Don't go easy on her. Challenge her and tell her what she needs to do better.
2. Give her a forum to defend herself and her ideas in front of others.

3. Use data as an unbiased measure of ideas and abilities, and provide the training necessary for employees to work comfortably with it.
4. If you make her cry, give her space to regroup.
5. Make sure you also tell her what she does well.

THE CEO PERSPECTIVE: BIG IDEAS FOR COMPANY-WIDE IMPACT

Meetup: Intentional Meeting Protocols to Ensure Every Voice Is Heard

Challenging people on the substance of their ideas can only happen when you actually hear everyone's ideas. At Meetup, CEO David Siegel designed a meeting protocol that ensures that every idea is brought to the surface. Meetup is a technology company that connects people with shared interests to create local communities and events. In some ways, Meetup looks like a typical tech company, with most of its operations happening online and a significant portion of its staff in technical roles. Yet the company far exceeds industry averages for female representation. On average, the employee population at US technology companies is 30 percent female. The percentages are even lower for technical roles, and for leadership roles.[8] At Meetup, 46 percent of its workforce is female, and 40 percent of its technical roles are held by women. Perhaps most impressively, 50 percent of its executive team is female.

Siegel attributes this success to deliberate actions taken at a company level, starting with a fundamental belief that having diverse representation across teams is valuable to business decision-making, policy setting, and the employee experience. "You need to internalize the business value that having a diverse team really matters," Siegel says. "If you go about it as an exercise of checking boxes, it will remain superficial. You have to really believe it and build it in to your everyday actions."

One way that Meetup does this is by formalizing business meeting protocols. Many women struggle to be heard in meetings, or to have their ideas given equal attention and consideration, particularly in environments that are dominated by men. In his previous role as CEO of Investopedia, which had a 70 percent male workforce, Siegel saw that dynamic clearly. Beyond the gender imbalance, Siegel felt that the traditional meeting format of unstructured conversation created an unfair advantage for extroverts over introverts. He wanted to ensure that those who are more thoughtful but less vocal could have the opportunity to strengthen their voice in the conversations. So, he created a different kind of meeting protocol at Investopedia, which worked so well that he later brought it to Meetup.

Here's how it works: for every strategy meeting, the team creates and contributes to a shared Google Doc in advance, to present all ideas related to the meeting topic and to establish a record of who suggested each idea. The team then generates the agenda directly from that document, so that the discussion at the meeting is based entirely on what was contributed in advance. This structure takes advocacy for ideas out of the dynamic of large meetings, which tend to reward louder voices or those quicker to jump in over another. It benefits all employees by creating more thoughtful, purposeful discussions with more of the individual thought work done in advance of the meeting, so that everyone's time can be used efficiently. Women in the company in particular have given feedback to the leadership that they feel this structure is beneficial to them.

It also gives credit where credit is due. Much has been written about the tendency of men to reclaim ideas initially offered by women in meetings. In 2017, physics professor

Nicole Gugliucci crystallized the concept when she introduced the phrase "hepeated" on Twitter, defining it as "when a woman suggests an idea and it's ignored, but then a guy says the same thing and everyone loves it."[9] The Meetup protocol addresses that challenge directly. Because the document tracks the flow of who wrote each item, and when they wrote it, credit is more accurately attributed to the individual who first introduced an idea, not to the one who said it the loudest.

One key to success is simply sticking to the protocol once established. "Our rule is that if you don't comment in the doc, you're not allowed to show up at the meeting," Siegel explains. "Everyone has the opportunity to add their thoughts in advance. The purpose of the meeting is not to bring up new information. You have to be fairly stringent about enforcing the rules to truly change behavior."

Use of this meeting structure has created a more comfortable work environment for women. It ensures that every voice is heard and that the best ideas make it to every conversation, which in turn leads to better decision-making for the company.

The Big Idea

Establish meeting protocols to ensure that every voice is heard.

Why It Works

- Provides a forum for idea sharing that does not require competing for airtime.
- Gives credit where credit is due.
- Rewards advance planning.
- Neutralizes more aggressive advocacy for ideas.

RULE #9

TELL HER THAT YOU SEE HER POTENTIAL

Just as she was going out on maternity leave from her university academic position, Carol, an entrepreneur and CEO, had a career crisis. She had hit a major roadblock in her academic career. A standoff with a senior colleague in her department left her in a situation where she was not going to get the tenured position she had been expecting. After some tears, she regrouped and started interviewing for a new job, only six weeks after her daughter was born. She pursued an opportunity at the Brown Women Writers Project and was offered a product manager position in the Center for Electronic Texts and Humanities, a think tank at Princeton. She accepted the position, but she was still struggling.

"I was really twisted around that I hadn't gotten tenure, feeling like the bottom had fallen out and I was a failure. I just couldn't get over it. My boss, Susan, pulled me aside, and she said, 'Look. You can do just about anything. You have a PhD from Princeton University. I have a lot of things that have your name on them, but I can't hold your hand. I'm going to hand them off; you're going to figure out what you know and what you don't know. You can come back and ask me questions, and if I know and can mentor you I will; otherwise, I will send you to find what you don't know. I have hired you to figure things out.'"

Those words jolted Carol into action. "Then, I got to pitch Microsoft and apply for NEH grants and NSF grants, and I got to put together global conferences. Susan remade me as somebody who could build edtech products. She took this weepy, sad person—I had just had a baby, my clothes didn't fit—and she told me, 'Lots of women have done much harder things than this. You can do this.' And then she would just give me stuff. And I figured it out."

The best type of validation is not just complimenting her on a job well done; it's identifying the future potential you see in her based on the strengths that you see in her. So, when you see a chance for her to stretch herself, and you think she will rise to the occasion, tell her. Tell her that you think it's a great opportunity for her and why she can do it. Connect the skills you see in her to the opportunity and show her your confidence in her abilities. Better yet, offer her an opportunity that will stretch her or take her in a new direction.

Offer Stretch Opportunities

Melissa, a CFO, worked in finance for the first decade of her career, specializing in the pharmaceutical industry. She hadn't seriously thought about leaving finance for an operating role, and she certainly hadn't openly expressed interest in that to anyone. But when her twin sister's boss* was leaving his job at a large company to launch a pharmaceutical startup, he needed a CFO to partner with him, and he thought of her. He had met Melissa through her sister, and he knew she had strong financial skills and a passion for pharma. So he reached out and asked her if she would consider leaving her job at a hedge fund to come start a new company with him.

For Melissa, this was the chance to take her career in a completely new direction, and she was really intrigued by the opportunity. She wasn't 100 percent sure that she would be a good CFO, or that she would enjoy it, but there were a lot of reasons to believe that she would. So she made the leap and joined him. Working in a fast-paced startup environment, she had a lot of autonomy to figure things out and use her judgment. It turned out, she loved being a CFO, and they built something very successful together. Today, she is the CFO of a publicly traded pharmaceutical company. Reflecting back, she says, "If Demetrios hadn't given me that opportunity and

---

* Melissa's twin sister is a physician and also works in the pharmaceutical industry, so it's not so random that her boss made this connection!

taken that chance on me, I don't know if I would have had the career I've ended up having as a CFO."

Entrepreneurial environments can be ideal for women to develop and stretch their skills because there are fewer constraints and expectations around what any given role should look like and what background is appropriate for it. Jake, an entrepreneur and founding CEO of several companies, has found that in the earlier stages of building a company, he can offer roles that individuals might not have direct experience for, but they have the talent to excel in the role. "In earlier stages you can take more risks on people. Later on, investors start saying things like, 'We need more gray hair on the executive team,' which doesn't necessarily favor women. I was able to give big roles to women with potential in the early years of growing my company. One of those women in particular was tremendously successful, and now she is the founding CEO of a new company that I'm backing."

Offering stretch opportunities works—but you may need to push her to see herself in such a role. In Rule #2, Be Someone She Can Relate To, I addressed why having relatable role models helps employees envision themselves in leadership roles. It's difficult to picture yourself being successful at something when you've never seen anyone like you do it before. I was lucky: I was able to find and go to work for a very literal role model in Mandy, a woman who I could emulate in lots of ways. We can't count on that happening for every talented woman in the workplace, but we can do a better job of helping every woman envision herself in a more powerful position by making the connections for her when they aren't as obvious as they were for me with Mandy.

Years before I met Mandy, I had a conversation about becoming a CEO that went very differently. I had been running the mergers and acquisitions (M&A) team at Kaplan for many years when the leader of the company's largest division, Jeff, offered me an opportunity to leave my corporate job to come run a business within his division. To really have an impact at a company, he argued, I needed to generate profits, and I could learn how to do that in the role he was offering. It was a risk he was taking; when you give someone a business to run with no prior experience, there's a chance they will lose a lot of money. But it was a risk he was willing to take on me.

I very quickly dismissed the idea. "I'm a deal person," I protested. "I buy companies; I don't run them. I should stick to what I'm good at."

Jeff paused, and then asked me, "What do you see yourself doing in ten years? Because I think you're going to be a great CEO one day."

I responded almost reflexively, "Oh no, I don't see myself becoming a CEO." The idea felt far-fetched to me.

"Well, what do you see yourself becoming?" he prodded.

I thought and then responded, "I could see becoming a really strong number two in an organization, taking someone's vision and really executing well to make it happen."

I've thought a lot about why my perspective on becoming a CEO was so different when I discussed my career potential with Jeff, compared with my feelings about it five years later when I worked for Mandy. Mandy wasn't just a good boss for me; I also had a lot in common with her. We were both working mothers with two daughters each, and we both had earned MBAs.* So when Mandy said to me, "I see you as the next CEO," it wasn't that hard for me to picture

---

* We even looked alike. Early in the days after we merged Tutor.com with The Princeton Review, I attended the corporate holiday party for our Boston office, and Mandy couldn't make it. Employees had seen our leadership team on video screens many times for company meetings, but many had not yet spent time in person with us. About an hour in, sitting around a table chatting with a captive audience, someone called me Mandy, and I realized that everyone thought I was her. Apparently, we looked so similar on video that they mixed us up in real life.

myself following in her footsteps. Whereas when Jeff said it, I just couldn't see it.

I had fifteen years of experience in the workplace prior to meeting Mandy. I had met many strong, smart, successful female role models over those years. But none of them were CEOs. The CEOs of all the companies I worked with were men. In the first decade of my career, I was often the only woman in the room. I had never interacted with a female CEO; powerful women existed in my corporate sphere, but they were chief administrative officers, chief operating officers, or chiefs of staff, all supporting male CEOs. In hindsight, of course when Jeff asked me in 2009 who I saw myself becoming, I thought I would become a strong number two in an organization. Based on the role models I had been watching, those were the women that I could relate to, emulate, and aspire to become.

I needed help expanding my imagination to be able to see the potential when it was not evident to me in my own experiences. When offering a stretch opportunity to someone who has less in common with you or the other role models she sees, you may have to push more than once to get her to envision the potential that you are seeing in her.

Engage in a Conversation About Her Future Goals

Career development is not just about immediate opportunities; it's about telling a woman you see a promising path for her. After becoming a CEO, I noticed a trend inside my own company: female employees, at all levels and roles, started scheduling time with me to tell me about their ambition and to ask about ways to develop their careers. It was such a pronounced trend that it couldn't have been the case that all that ambition suddenly materialized. It was there, but it was hidden, and nobody was noticing it or doing anything about it. When I came along, these women could relate to me and they finally felt comfortable saying out loud what they wanted for their careers. It didn't feel so hard to tell me, a young female CEO, what they aspired to become.

Once I started hearing all these requests for support and development, I knew that I needed to get better training in place. Even if you aren't the CEO or in a position to create your own budget for training, you'll find that most HR departments have some budget set aside for management and skills training and that you will be able to advocate for approval to fund training for your team if you ask.

Now, whenever I'm mentoring a young woman, I make it a practice to ask her which C-suite job she wants to have in the future. Not just, where do you see yourself in the future? What's the end goal, the big job that you want to get to? More often than not, she is pleasantly surprised to receive the question, but she doesn't struggle to answer. Women are thinking about these paths and which future jobs they can do well; they just don't know that their bosses see them that way too. I recommend that every manager have this conversation. Ask your direct reports which C-suite job they envision for themselves, and if they struggle to see it, help to create the vision by telling them where you see their potential.

Jerin, a sales manager, started out her career in customer success. She knew that she performed well and was very skilled at cultivating client relationships, yet when a new job opening came up at her company for a higher-paying field sales role, she did not initially apply.

"When that role came up, I had all the confidence in my abilities to step into the role and rise to the occasion," recalled Jerin, "but I was hitting my stride in customer success and many of my colleagues were tenured salespeople. I didn't know if my boss would consider me for the transition into field sales."

The story might have ended there. But Jerin's boss, Sandi, was thinking proactively about talent development on her team, and she saw potential in Jerin. Sandi had hoped that Jerin would apply for the sales role, and when she didn't, Sandi didn't just write her off as not ready or not interested. She sought her out to tell her that she thought she should apply. "Jerin was clearly a rising star in her role in customer success, but I am always seeking the right talent for new business sales. Sales skills like discovery and closing can be taught, but what cannot be taught is authenticity, passion, the ability to build rapport and integrity. As a sales leader, I recognized all these qualities in Jerin."

Sandi conveyed her confidence in Jerin's ability to perform the job well, and she initiated a conversation about a multiyear career trajectory for Jerin, envisioning a move to the sales role as the next step on the way to a role in sales management. "As a manager, it is my responsibility to invest in my team members and provide them with growth opportunities. In Jerin's case, just a little nudge is all she needed."

"It was not only exactly the encouragement that I needed to pursue it, but it was a testament to the company I worked for and the strong leadership and support I had," recalls Jerin. "I appreciated being at a place that saw me not just for the work I was producing at the time, but for what I could grow into over time."

Any manager, male or female, can act as Sandi did in this case. Understand the career goals for everyone on your team, and when you see opportunities for them to develop and advance, seek them out and encourage them to stretch. Don't assume "She didn't apply, so maybe she doesn't want the extra responsibility." That assumption can easily be checked by asking. Ask her if it's something she's interested in, and tell her if you think she should apply. She'll appreciate the engagement in her career development.

Also rest assured that doing this doesn't create an obligation for you. If she's one of many applicants, tell her that it will be a competitive process and you think it's important for her to try. You can encourage her to apply without creating an expectation that she will automatically get the job. It's about introducing the opportunity to stretch her skills and experience.

The Myth of the Confidence Gap

There is an often-cited statistic that men apply for jobs where they meet 60 percent of the stated qualifications, whereas women only apply to jobs where they meet 100 percent of the requirements. These numbers come from a 2004 internal review of job listings and applications at Hewlett-Packard, a large enterprise with data on sixty thousand employees.[1] The myth that has spread based on that statistic is that men have more confidence in their ability to perform.

But the problem women face is not a lack of confidence in their own skills. A *Harvard Business Review* follow-up to the HP study surveyed men and women who considered but did not apply to various job listings.[2] The survey asked them why they didn't apply, providing a list of possible reasons. For both genders, the least often selected response was "I didn't think I could do the job well"; 12 percent of men and 10 percent of women selected that explanation. This sheds a new light on confidence; women are not saying that they don't believe they can do it.

The response that was highest for both men and women was "I didn't think they would hire me since I don't meet the qualifications." Reluctance to apply for a job connects with the employee's belief about how the hiring manager will perceive their candidacy. Women have good reason to believe that people are less likely to hire them if they don't have the perfect resume that checks all the boxes. So, when they opt out of applying, it's a practical decision, not a reflection of their self-confidence.

Another study analyzed data from an unnamed large, male-dominated technology company and found that being perceived as confident did not lead to equal job success for men and women. While for men there was a direct correlation between being perceived as confident and receiving raises and promotions, this was not true for women. For women to receive raises and promotions, they needed to score high on two measures: confidence and perceived caring for others. If the women weren't perceived as caring individuals who placed the priorities of others over themselves, they weren't successful.[3]

A *Harvard Business Review* article called out the implications of this perception gap for women: "Popular messaging about how women must change to appear more self-confident as a key to their success isn't just false. It also reflects how the burden of managing a gender-diverse workplace is placed on the female employees themselves. Where their male colleagues are allowed to focus on their own objectives, women who are expected to care for others are shouldering an unfair load."[4]

This again highlights the flaw of advising women to find success by acting more like men. It doesn't work for them. Managers leave women to their own devices when they tell them to act with more confidence. Women know that if they do that, they will also have to figure out how to offset the perception of that confidence with just the right amount of caring and kindness. They will have to add sugar to the medicine to get their colleagues to accept it.

When that opportunity for promotion comes up, remember this context. She may worry, and with good reason according to the data, that if she applies without being 100 percent qualified, her confidence will offend people and she will be penalized for it. If she doesn't think she'll be seriously considered for the role anyway, she may decide it isn't worth the risk to apply. Remember the story of Jerin and Sandi. If you'd like to see her apply for a promotion, even if she's not 100 percent qualified on paper, encourage her to do so. You don't have to leave it to her to demonstrate her ambition by coming forward and applying. There could be all kinds of reasons holding her back from applying that have nothing to do with ambition or ability.

Don't Tell Her to Be More Confident; Show Her That You Recognize Her Capabilities

Managers often tell women that they need to project a more confident air, not just when applying for jobs but throughout their work. Be more confident, and you will find success. But remember, the research shows that she doesn't have a confidence problem. The problem is in her estimation of what you really think of her.

Don't perpetuate the myth of the female confidence problem by telling your female direct reports that they need to be more confident in themselves. Calling something a confidence issue when it's not just gives her a new reason to worry that you don't think highly of her. You create a new problem when you perceive and declare self-doubt to be there when it's not. Instead, help them to be more confident in their reputations by showing them the evidence of the positive perceptions you and others have of their performance.

My very first performance review was a three-month check-in with my staffer Dave at Goldman Sachs, to discuss how I was doing in my first months as an investment banking analyst. Dave was responsible for aggregating the performance feedback from all my individual project managers. What resulted was a very comprehensive and honest report of what the people I worked for thought my work. The feedback was very positive. My work was well perceived and my skills, especially my financial modeling skills, were rated above average. It was an exciting meeting for me, listening to him read out direct quotes from my various managers, giving me specific insight into what they thought of my work.

I was surprised by the review because I had expected it to be worse. I didn't know that all these people I worked with thought as highly of me as they actually did. If we had ended the review there, it would have been great. But then Dave said to me, "You know, you're doing a better job than you think you are. You should have more confidence in yourself." He meant well, but that comment stung. It made me feel like the flaw was in *me*; to have a strong future at the firm, I needed to project more confidence in myself. Until that moment, I didn't lack confidence in myself. I knew that my work was above average. What I didn't know was if my managers also saw that.

His feedback made me more worried about my future instead of helping me to be more confident. I wondered, *Why does he think that I don't think I'm doing a good job? What am I doing wrong that makes people think I don't have confidence in my work?* If instead he had altered his feedback to "You should feel great. Your work is solid and these reviews clearly show that your managers are confident in the work you're producing," I would have walked away on cloud nine. But instead of feeling good, I walked away questioning more than ever if this was the right place for me to be successful. In addition to working hard and producing great work, I also needed to figure out how to show people that I was confident in my work. That felt hard.

Be careful when you give an employee feedback. If you believe she doesn't fully appreciate how highly others think of her, focus on correcting that perception. Don't confuse it by suggesting or assuming that this is happening because she lacks self-confidence.

I once received an email from a young and talented employee who was leaving our company to pursue an opportunity with another company. He left on good terms, and he wrote in his farewell email to me, "You're a really talented and inspiring CEO. I don't know if you know that, so I wanted to tell you." I knew that he had good intentions, and it was a very nice note. But if his goal was to give me more confidence, this note did not accomplish that. He left me wondering, *Why would he think that I don't know that I'm a good CEO? Do I come across as lacking confidence?* If he had instead said, "I don't know if you know how much people at the company value having you as our CEO," it would have been a much more empowering note for me. I was a new CEO, so I didn't know if everyone at the company felt that way about me. It would have been great to be told that they did. The gap that needed filling had nothing to do with my feelings about myself; it was a gap in the insight I had into the perceptions of my team. Think about this whenever you have opportunities to give feedback to the women on your team. It's not about what she thinks of herself; it's about making sure she has an accurate read on what others think of her.

Understanding Her Perspective: What a Good Boss Needs to Know

1. She doesn't lack confidence in herself, but she may lack confidence in how you, her boss, perceive her.
2. She is unlikely to put herself forward for opportunities that she doesn't meet 100 percent of the criteria for.
3. She's thinking about future opportunities and will be excited to talk about it if you ask her.
4. She can see through compliments that do more to elevate the giver than they do to highlight her skills and capabilities.

When a Compliment Isn't Really a Compliment

Conventional wisdom would say that "everybody loves a compliment." But not every compliment is created equal. Give compliments of substance, not compliments about appearance or style. And make sure that the compliments you give are genuinely for her benefit, and that they serve to lift her up, not to elevate your own status.

When I first became CEO of The Princeton Review, I was thirty-nine years old, and I looked at least five years younger than that. I quickly learned that people have expectations of what a CEO should look like, and I wasn't it. Nearly everyone who didn't know me was surprised to learn that I was the CEO of a nationally known company, and they visibly struggled to react appropriately. Some of their reactions illustrate the difference between a good compliment and a bad compliment.

The women, especially younger women, wouldn't necessarily hide their surprise. But they would say admiring things like, "Wow, that's amazing!" or "That's really impressive!" They would ask about how I found success and what advice I had for them. I generally left those interactions with my confidence boosted, feeling like an admired role model.

Men, on the other hand, most often had one of two reactions. Some would say, "You look so young to be a CEO!" Some would say that telling someone they look young is a compliment. But context matters. This type of compliment is off base in a professional context. If someone at my gym wants to tell me how young I look, they are welcome to, but at a business meeting it falls flat. In business, young equals inexperienced, which equals not qualified for the job. At least that's how I took it.

The other type of compliment I received from men, especially older men, was to smile and say, "Good for you!" This "compliment" felt condescending. Complimenting me with the same phrase one might use to compliment a child who successfully solves a puzzle downgraded my accomplishment and my importance as an individual. The statement presumed that somehow the speaker of the phrase had the superiority to validate my career success. This especially bothered me when the people who said it weren't even CEOs themselves.

Essentially, some of the compliments that men give women don't really feel like compliments. There's a name for this: "benevolent sexism." Benevolent sexism happens when on the surface a man is giving a compliment to a woman, but in fact he is undermining her. There are two ways he might be undermining her: either by complimenting an attribute that is not really relevant to the professional topic at hand, or by suggesting that he is in a position to compliment her at all.

David Mayer's article "How Not to Advocate for a Woman at Work" expands on this point.[5] In the article he dissects a CNN interview from 2017 in which then White House communications director Anthony Scaramucci spoke about then Press Secretary Sarah Huckabee Sanders in highly complimentary terms, focusing in particular on her "warm" style and her appearance. "Sarah," Scaramucci said on air, "if you're watching, I loved the hair and makeup person we had on Friday." The author posited that Scaramucci had done Huckabee Sanders a disservice by complimenting her. By complimenting her personality and appearance, he was highlighting nonprofessional attributes that did not speak to her competence in the role the way that a compliment about her intelligence or charisma would have.

In the interview, Scaramucci discusses how great Huckabee Sanders is doing, and how he will continue to work to "make her better." This is another example of a compliment having a negative effect. By suggesting that he is in a position to opine on her performance, Scaramucci is actually taking himself up a notch, which in turn brings her down. Offering to help someone improve, or validating how well they are doing, can do more harm than good.

Even if on the surface something seems like a nice thing to say, you need to think about the context. Does she want your opinion? Does your opinion matter? Are you saying it to make yourself feel good or to make her feel good? Is your positive feedback related to a skill or capability that you yourself would want someone to associate you with in a work environment? A misplaced compliment takes the power away from the woman and gives it to the man to validate that, yes, in fact she's good.

Don't Just Tell Her That She Has Potential—Insist That She Does

When you tell a woman that she has potential, be as specific as you can be—what kinds of roles do you think she should be aiming for? What do you see in her that she might not yet see in herself? And remember, if she doesn't react with wholehearted enthusiasm the first time you tell her, that doesn't get you off the hook for having tried. There can be a lot of assumptions holding women back, so if you can find a way to ask more than once, keep trying to help women see themselves in ways they hadn't yet thought about.

When Ann McDaniel was the managing editor of *Newsweek*, Don Graham, the CEO of the magazine's parent company, The Washington Post Company, tapped her to join the corporate executive team. Her first reaction to taking on a new opportunity was to back away, believing that she wasn't qualified to do the job. "I said I was uniquely unqualified for management. I had no experience, and no idea if I could do it well. Don said, 'I have two reasons why I know you can do this. Number one, you've shown yourself to have very good judgment, and number two, you have a willingness to speak truth to power.'

"Just saying that to me gave me the courage to tell him what I thought, to challenge when I disagreed, and to admit mistakes. We had a very successful working relationship. Because we both cared equally, and we were out to benefit the company, we could argue in favor of something knowing that it came from respect, hard work, passion. It's the right thing for any organization to have managers who collaborate with their people. Two minds are often better than one."

There are so many obstacles that hold women back from reaching their full potential at work. As a manager, you have the ability to eliminate many of them, and the easiest of all are the ones that simply require you to tell her what you think. Don't let any of the women on your team limit their ambition because they don't know or see what's possible. There's nothing more powerful or impactful than telling someone that you think they are capable of great things.

Good Boss Checklist: What You Can Do to Be a Better Boss for Women

1. Make sure she knows where you see her potential.
2. Create opportunities or encourage her to apply for promotions that will stretch her.
3. Insist that she take risks to achieve her potential.
4. Give compliments, but give the right compliments. Highlight the strength of her skills and her work product.

THE CEO PERSPECTIVE: BIG IDEAS FOR COMPANY-WIDE IMPACT

ShopRunner: Supercharge Internal Promotions with Executive Coaching

Internet entrepreneur Sam Yagan has founded and grown multiple successful companies, including OkCupid and Spark-Notes. Over the course of doing so, he learned that having diverse leadership teams leads to better results. So, when he came to ShopRunner as its CEO in 2016, he knew that he wanted to bring more diversity to his executive team. He also believes that it's always better to source diversity from within via internal promotions, so that's the path he followed.

"I try to bias toward promotion from within whenever possible. Once you make diversity a priority, you have to be willing to be creative," says Yagan. "To identify people who aren't perfect candidates on paper and ask what's the right next step for them. Sometimes it's a promotion to put someone in a role that they're not technically qualified for; there's a place for that. Giving people opportunities out of their comfort zone can be incredibly effective. Other times it's being creative in new role creation. Create something that will give that person the access and experience that they need to grow.

"I have often made up roles to get someone in the position that I think will be best for both them and the company. I believe in being creative in the role, title, and responsibility to design exactly what I think someone needs to reach their full potential. To elevate people to their potential, you just need to be clear about your vision for what they can become. Be explicit in saying, 'This is my plan for you.'"

At ShopRunner, Yagan hired and promoted an entirely new team of executives, creating a team of six including himself. Three out of the five executives that report to him are women. Knowing that the new team needed to quickly come together and form its working norms, he brought in an executive coach to work with them. It was so beneficial to their process that he continued working with the coach on his own, and also offered to provide ongoing individualized coaching services to everyone on his team.

"More of the women have taken me up on that offer than the men," he reflected. Not only is coaching a great way to pinpoint the specific skills needed to ensure success, it facilitates a more direct kind of feedback and honest conversations between bosses and their direct reports. "We have conversations that we never would have without the executive coach." The addition of the executive coaching resources completes the support system, putting talented individuals into stretch roles that they have potential to grow into, and pairing that with the coaching to improve the chance of success. Together, internal promotions and executive coaching have been a winning formula for creating a diverse team at ShopRunner.

The Big Idea

Pair internal promotions with executive coaching.

Why It Works

- Sources talent from within.
- Gives bigger opportunity to proven talent with potential.
- De-risks the likelihood of success by supporting efforts with coaching.
- Strengthens the team dynamics to create a positive working environment.

CONCLUSION

The goal of this book is to make things easier. To make it easier for women to work, by removing the unnecessary distractions and unfair assumptions, and the disadvantages they create. And, to make it easier for managers to help, by showing them how to make small changes that add up to a big impact.

You're now equipped to frame your actions as a manager with an understanding of a woman's perspective: what she's going through, and how she's seeing and experiencing the workplace environment. And you now know to pair that with consideration for where she wants to get to: her goals and her potential.

With that context, you can take the right actions to be a good boss for the women you manage. Now that you better understand how the women on your team experience setbacks, frustrations, and obstacles at work, you can try to reduce, eliminate, or counteract them. When you do that, it will ease the path for her to reach her goals. It's that simple.

A new manager came into my office to talk to me about a hiring decision. She had been interviewing candidates to replace an employee who had recently left. I wanted her to hire one person in particular, but she had someone different in mind.

"My concern," she told me, "is that the guy you want me to hire seems pretty introverted, and that doesn't necessarily fit with my working style. The last person in this role had a very similar style to mine, and we accomplished a ton because it was just so easy and seamless to work together. I think it will go better if I hire someone like her again."

"Well," I responded, "I don't believe that you get to have a single working style when you're a manager. You need to adapt to what each person needs from you to be successful. This could be an opportunity for you to grow as a manager."

She gave in and hired the person that I preferred. She acknowledged later that it was valuable to push herself to expand her comfort zone as a manager. She took a step to improve her ability to work with all kinds of individuals, not just those who were easy, natural fits.

To promote diverse representation across teams, it's important for all managers to embrace the responsibility to work with all types of people. Managers don't get to pick only a certain type of person that they like to manage. We don't leave it to female managers to take responsibility for all the women at work; everyone is on the hook. Every manager needs to figure out how to adapt, respond to, and support the needs of all his or her direct reports. Following the nine rules in this book is a good first step.

The Work That Only Business Leaders Can Do

While the primary focus of this book is on ways that every single manager can support women, there is some work that needs to be assigned directly to the people who influence the structure of organizations: boards, investors, CEOs, and heads of HR. While managers are working hard to bend and shape the workplace to be more hospitable to women, we can't forget the primary reason that the workplace is unhospitable to them: there aren't enough women in positions of influence. The workplace wasn't made for women, it wasn't designed by women, and there aren't enough women with the power to change that dynamic.

Many of the environmental obstacles that exist for women in the workplace are there because it's predominantly men who are setting the examples. There are too few examples for women to emulate. There aren't enough women to recognize the potential in other women. More gender representation at the top is the most foolproof way to change that. The best way to help more women reach the C-suite is to put more women in the C-suite now. Boards need to advocate for female CEOs. CEOs need to put women on their executive teams. As of this writing, less than one-quarter of Fortune 500 board members are women.[1] Two-thirds of venture capital firms don't have a single female partner.[2] As companies, funds, and boards continue to prioritize gender rebalancing, the chance that high-potential women will find relatable role models is at least increasing. But what about all the high-potential individuals for whom it's even harder to find representation at senior levels? There are currently only three CEOs in the Fortune 500 who are persons of color,[3] and none of them are women. And 81 percent of venture firms don't have a single Black investor,[4] let alone a partner.

So, there is still much work to be done. Progress will accelerate as more boards and leadership teams enact systemic change from the top. But in the meantime, every manager, at any level, can have a positive impact on the careers of the women who work for them.

The Work Every Manager Can Do

My hope is that the nine simple rules outlined in this book will help every manager be a better boss for women. My additional hope is that someone else will write a version of this book on behalf of other underrepresented groups in the workplace. Following this framework of understanding perspective and then identifying small changes that add up to a bigger impact, we can enhance everyone's understanding of how the workplace is experienced differently, and what we all can do to make it a more welcoming environment for everyone.

Summary Checklist: Nine Ways You Can Support Women at Work

Rule #1: Call Her by Her Name
Rule #2: Be Someone She Can Relate To
Rule #3: Don't Ask, "What Does Your Husband Do?"
Rule #4: Don't Sit in Her Chair
Rule #5: Watch the Clock
Rule #6: Speak Up So That She Doesn't Have To
Rule #7: Don't Make Her Ask Twice
Rule #8: Be an Equal Opportunity Asshole
Rule #9: Tell Her That You See Her Potential

Rule #1: Call Her by Her Name

Get her name right. Spell it correctly, pronounce it correctly, and don't make a nickname out of it. Get her name right even if she gets married and changes it. Don't share your opinion on whether or not she should change it and what she changes it to. Oh, and don't call her sweetheart.

Rule #2: Be Someone She Can Relate To

You don't have to be a woman to relate to a woman. You just have to be an authentic human, who takes interest in others and shares something about your life outside of the office. Everyone has things in their life that they care about, and talking about these things helps to find common connecting points. All of that serves to make work relationships more real.

Rule #3: Don't Ask, "What Does Your Husband Do?"

Too often, people downgrade the ambition of women as they move through significant life events, particularly marriage and mother-hood. Don't make your own assumptions about how hard she wants to work, if and when she will have children, how much she cares about or needs income, and whether or not she will prioritize family over work. Assume that she continues to have ambition and wants bigger opportunities, until and unless she tells you otherwise.

Rule #4: Don't Sit in Her Chair

Prepare for a woman's return from maternity leave. Reclaim and organize her physical office space and belongings. Protect her proj-ects and her stapler from office vultures. Respect the time, space, and privacy she will need for nursing. Be thoughtful about quickly reengaging her in substantive work.

Rule #5: Watch the Clock

Working moms typically have to account for every hour of their day, and there is little margin for error. Respect the start and the end of the day. Wherever possible, allow for flexibility in letting women choose which hours of the day they work. Unless you have reason for concern, trust that the work is getting done even if it's happening out of your view.

Rule #6: Speak Up So That She Doesn't Have To

Even in today's more evolved workplace, people say inappropriate things to women. A good boss tells them to stop. A strong manager insists on respectful behavior toward the women on their team and takes the burden off the woman from having to deal with it on her own.

Rule #7: Don't Make Her Ask Twice

It is risky for women to negotiate. You stack the odds meaningfully against women when you set up dynamics on your teams that require people to aggressively self-advocate. Instead, proactively offer raises and promotions before she has to ask.

Rule #8: Be an Equal Opportunity Asshole

Being tough on a woman and pushing her to be better at her job can be a good thing and shows that you believe she's worth the effort. Especially if you give her the skills and the forum to defend her ideas. But if you make her cry, try to be cool about it. And try not to make her cry.

Rule #9: Tell Her That You See Her Potential

Envision a bigger future for her and tell her. Tell her why she's capable and put her in positions that allow her to do more. Give her time to prepare and time to react. Give compliments that bolster her, not you.

There are all kinds of managers and all kinds of management styles. *The Good Boss* has shown many different ways to support women, things that anyone can do, no matter what your style. Changing the environment for women starts with their day-to-day experiences. Everything that you do to smooth out that experience has an impact that can make the difference between a woman advancing in her career or being held back. Being a good boss for women is the right thing to do. It's also the smart thing to do. It's the responsibility of everyone, male or female. If every manager commits to doing their part to improve the workplace for women, it will add up to a fundamentally changed structure that works better for everyone.

ACKNOWLEDGMENTS

Countless colleagues and more than two decades of work experiences contributed to the making of this book. My perspective is informed by all these interactions, large and small. Many contributors generously shared their stories and experiences with me and are cited in the book. I also want to say a special thank-you to those who shared their stories with anonymity. It is still brave and generous to tell your story without naming names, and to hope that in doing so you will change the circumstances for women in the future.

The Good Boss, and the career experiences that it is based on, has been immeasurably impacted by Mandy Ginsberg, my own good boss. Without Mandy, I am not sure that I ever would have become a CEO, and I am certain that I wouldn't be the kind of CEO that I am. Mandy is the ultimate model of a good boss and I continue to depend on her mentorship.

This book would also not exist without Carol Barash, who helped me unearth and shape the book that I wanted to write. She taught me how to bring out the best parts of my own stories and how to write the stories of others.

Thank you to the many people who contributed to this work:

My agent, Johanna Castillo, for taking a chance on a first-time writer and believing that people would want to read my book, because she genuinely wanted to read my book. And thank you to Sarah Branham for helping me find her.

The team at BenBella. In my very first conversation with Glenn Yeffeth and Leah Wilson, I felt I had found the team that understands what I'm trying to say and wants to amplify my message. I appreciate so many rewarding and productive months of work with Claire Schulz, my editor, who made my writing sharper and better without ever making it feel like it wasn't coming from me. I'm grateful for the energy of everyone else on the team who has put so much thought and creativity into what this book is and how we have brought it to readers.

My own good bosses: Johan de Muinck Keizer, Don Graham, Jonathan Grayer, and Gerry Rosberg, for indelibly impacting my career trajectory and for creating work connections that felt like family. Greg Blatt and, again, Mandy Ginsberg for seeing my potential and taking a leap of faith on me as a first-time CEO. Mia Hegazy, Brian Rich, and Gene Wolfson, for showing me, and giving me room to show them, that I had found the right company to lead next.

Thank you also to my other bosses. I have changed some names and identifying details, but their stories are in here, too, and are part of my journey. I am grateful for what each one taught me.

Thank you to the people who have trusted me to be their boss. Each has taught me something about how to be a good manager. Most especially Gabi Murphy, who improves upon everything I do and makes our work together always feel both meaningful and fun. And Anthony Pane, who has worked with me for the longest and who I can always count on to tell me the truth. To those who have been important parts of my teams in the past, who I hope to cross paths with again: Michelle Bergland, Sam Byun, Stacy Caldwell, Rob Franek, Sarah Hauser, Vincent Jungels, Paul Kanarek, Keiko Katsuragawa, Ryan Kiick, Anne Kofol Hogarty, Brooks Morgan, Phil Schwarz, Young Shin, Vanessa Soman, Candice Szu, Sandi White, and Scott Williams. To those who believed in me enough to double down on working for me again, knowing that loyalty and respect flow in both directions and that we do our best work when we do it together: Brian Culbreth, Yasmin Gamboa, Russ Greenspan, Jerin Jones, Stacey Milgram, Cecilia Retelle Zywicki, Laura Sullivan, and Brian Stephen. And to those I work closely with at PresenceLearning: Summer Allison, Piper Brown, Ashley DelPozzo, Cole Dudley, Sarah Finney, Eliza Kosanovich, Kristin Martinez, Jack Phillips, Lana Ratcliff, Shanelle Reese, Dara Rogoff, and Stephanie Taylor.

I wish that I could thank everyone who works at PresenceLearning by name, but that would be more than one thousand names! In addition to the team members I've named already, I want to say a special thank-you to my colleagues who have shared the powerful stories of their experiences as women of color, reminding me all over again why diversity and representation at work is so important, and that for all that white women have endured at work, the burden is infinitely heavier for Black women: Jenn Wilkins, Julia Gachet, and Shanelle Reese.

My brain trust of thoughtful male managers: Chris Eberle, Drew Geant, Stew Oldfield, Laurence Reszetar, Phil Schwarz, and Jake Schwartz—thank you for giving me the unfiltered male perspective, and for helping me focus my advice and make it relevant to men.

My collective of brilliant, ambitious, generous, inspiring professional women: Amy Calhoun Robb, Kristen Campbell, Elizabeth Chou, Michelle Dervan, Anna Edwards, Melissa Epperly, Sari Factor, Kate Haviland, Susan Herzog Lichtman, Beth Hollenberg, Shubha Hoveland, Jessica Kahan Dvorett, Anne Kuo Hyun, Bobbi Kurshan, Darria Long Gillespie, Lauren Marler Chewning, Andrea Mainelli, Molly McCarthy, MJ Miller, Cindy Myles Laegeler, Megan O'Connor, Jackie Ouellette DiLaura, Deborah Quazzo, Meredith Ruble, Kim Schaller Grant, Lorin Thomas Tavel, and Emma Watford. These women have served simultaneously as my role models, mentors, advisors, and support systems throughout my career.

My sister, Karyn, without whom I wouldn't have been able to do any of the work that formed the basis for this book. She has cared for my daughters with generosity and love, allowing me to leave my home for work every day without guilt, worry, or regret.

My husband, Chris, who told me with confidence every time I questioned whether I should continue working after we had our children that he simply could not imagine me stopping. Thank you for being an active contributor to our second shift, for changing jobs so that we could move back to New York for my job, and for working off a folding card table throughout our months at home during the pandemic, so that I could have full use of the fancy marble writing desk.

And last but never least, thank you to my daughters, Marion and Audrey, for reminding me what's most important, for giving me great ideas, and for thinking it's cool that your mom is a CEO. Others have questioned whether I'd be a better parent if I worked less, but you have never made me feel like anything other than exactly the right mom for you. You will be great bosses one day, and you already rule my world.

APPENDIX

HOW TO FIND *YOUR* GOOD BOSS

This book offers simple recommendations for managers who want to change the working environment for women, and it will serve to create more good bosses for women. But change takes time, so what about the women who are seeking to get ahead now? Until the day that all managers are good bosses, women need to find the ones who are.

So, if you don't yet have that good boss, how can you find one? Whether you're considering a new job opportunity or trying to decide whether your current job is right for you, there are signs and signals to look for to determine if you already have a good boss, if there's potential for your boss to become a good boss, or whether you should cut your losses because your boss will never be a good boss. Don't forget to look at yourself too: there are things that you can be doing to position yourself to connect with a good boss.

Here are twelve ways to improve your chances of finding your own good boss:

1. Demonstrate that you are worth investing in.
Good employees get good bosses. All the advice in this list is predicated upon being an employee worth investing in. Work hard and go

above and beyond what's expected of you. A good boss will only see your potential if you show it to them.

2. Be honest about who you are and what you need.
Your relationship with your boss is one of the most important ones in your life. You interact daily. Make sure you choose to spend that time as yourself. You should feel like your boss really knows you and is someone with whom you feel comfortable being your true self.

3. Choose someone who you can relate to.
You don't need to be just like your boss. Many of the strongest working relationships stem from bringing different perspectives to a decision. But you need to have enough in common to be able to have productive conversations. Find something you both care about and can connect on. Identify something in your boss that you also see in yourself and can emulate.

4. Like your boss.
Strong working relationships depend upon communication and access. You should enjoy spending time with your boss. You can usually tell from your very first conversation or interview if this is a person you like and enjoy talking to. If you don't, you may find yourself hiding when your boss walks by, relieved when they are out of the office traveling, or nervous when they come your way. It's very hard to have an active, open line of communication with someone you don't really like.

5. Listen when a trusted manager offers you an opportunity.
The most important choice you can make is to go work for the right person. It's much more important than the job title or what company you go to. So, when someone who knows you and has advocated for

you in the past offers you a new opportunity, take a good, long look at it, even if it seems hard or off the path you think you want to be on.

6. Believe the positive feedback you receive.

When someone tells you they see potential in you, listen. Ask for advice. Propose ideas. Don't just say thank you and walk away. Take it as an invitation to pursue bigger opportunities, learn new things, and take risks.

7. Be wary when someone defers promises to the future.

Be skeptical of job offers that involve a step down in job title or pay, with a promise that if everything goes well you'll get a bump up in the future. If a boss is unwilling to bet on you and elevate you on the way in the door, they are unlikely to become your strongest advocate later.

8. Find a boss who will push you forward.

If you see a new job opportunity in your company and wonder why no one thought of you, you probably don't have the right boss, because they should have recommended you for it. If you tell your boss you want to go for something and they tell you they don't think you're ready, you probably don't have the right boss, unless they provide you with clear reasons and steps you can take to become ready. If your boss tells you that you're too valuable and they just can't spare you to take on other, more interesting work, you definitely don't have the right boss.*

---

* Once, I suggested to a manager that he encourage a woman on his team to apply for a more advanced job in the company. He said he didn't want her to leave her current role for a few more months because she was doing essential work for him. I said, "That's not acceptable! Be a good boss and encourage her now; she's ready whether it suits your own timeline or not!"

9. Stick with someone who delivers without being asked.

Good bosses surprise on the upside in ways that you weren't expecting. They know how important it is to not only give praise for good work, but to put the company's money where its mouth is. If you've gone years in your job without your boss offering you something more that you didn't have to ask for (a raise, a bonus, a promotion), question it.

10. Find someone who you can learn from.

There were times where I felt like I could do the job of my boss better than they could. Those bosses never turned out to be my good bosses. You should feel like your boss knows what they are doing and that you can learn from their skills and experience.

11. A good boss gives credit generously.

Good employees consider it their job to make their boss look good. But the same should be true in reverse too. Good bosses make their employees look good. They give credit for high-quality work, not just by telling you it was great, but by telling others how great it was. They build your reputation for you by ensuring that others know when you've done something well. They never take individual credit for team efforts.

12. A good boss is a good listener.

If you find yourself repeating things you know you already said, maybe your boss is hearing you but not really listening. Signals that someone is not a good listener can come as early as the first introduction. Someone who gets your name wrong or forgets where you said you went to school or asks you the same question twice. Bad listeners can come in two forms: someone who doesn't really pay close attention to anyone or someone who only pays attention to people that he thinks are important. It doesn't really matter which of those types you're dealing with. If you're not being heard, you're not going to be seen for your full capabilities. Being a bad listener is a fatal flaw for a boss.

Once you've found that good boss that you want to go work for, don't get thrown off by the perils of negotiation. Negotiating job offers is hard, especially when it's a job that you really want. Tactics that work for men don't always work for women. Here are some strategies that do tend to work for women.

Advice for Women: Five Tips for Negotiating a Job Offer in Today's Imperfect System

1. Start by asking open questions instead of making direct requests. "Is there room for negotiation? Is this your best and final offer? Does this offer match the starting salary that my peers on the team received?" These questions help set a tone that is unapologetic and less personal, keeping the negotiation professional and unemotional.

2. Give options. Ask for more than one thing (higher base salary, bigger bonus potential, better job title, etc.) so that you allow your future boss to determine which parts to give. This will allow him to feel that he has "won" some parts of the negotiation. Importantly, though, make sure that when you ask for multiple things, you ask for them all at once.

Nobody likes it when they think they've delivered a good response only to be told there's "one more thing."

3. Convey your enthusiasm. As you negotiate, be very clear that you are excited about the job and the company, and that your efforts to be adequately paid for your value in no way should be interpreted as a lack of enthusiasm for the opportunity itself.

4. Don't settle for promises. If someone tries to kick the can down the road by saying that they can't give you more now but can adjust in the near future, be very cautious. If it's this easy to say no to your request for more salary now, it's quite possible that more excuses and delays will emerge once you are in the job.

5. Use the negotiation to evaluate your potential boss. If she or he doesn't react well to your negotiation and doesn't make you feel like you are valued, don't take the job. Not everyone is a good boss for women, and negotiations reveal true colors!

NOTES

Introduction

1. Michelle Fox, "Tackling the gender gap: 'Wall Street's been a boy's club forever,'" January 16, 2019, CNBC, www.cnbc.com/2019/01/16/women-on-wall-street-unequal-pay -and-fewer-female-advisors.

2. Minitab Blog Editor, "What Are the Odds? Chutes and Ladders," April 1, 2016, blog .minitab.com/blog/fun-with-statistics/what-are-the-odds-chutes-and-ladders.

3. McKinsey & Company and LeanIn.Org, "Women in the Workplace 2019," October 15, 2019, womenintheworkplace.com/.

4. Vanessa Fuhrmans, "Where Women Fall Behind at Work: The First Step into Management," *Wall Street Journal,* October 15, 2019, www.wsj.com/articles/where -women-fall-behind-at-work-the-first-step-into-management-11571112361.

5. Korn Ferry, "Women CEOs Speak: The CEO Pipeline Project," November 8, 2017, engage.kornferry.com/womenceosspeak.

6. Catalyst, "Women in Management: Quick Take," August 7, 2019, www.catalyst.org /research/women-in-management.

7. Phil Wahba, "Next Clorox boss will bring the number of Fortune 500 women CEOs to 38, highest yet," *Fortune,* August 3, 2020, fortune.com/2020/08/03/clorox-ceo-linda -rendle-fortune-500-women-ceos-all-time-high/; McKinsey & Company and LeanIn .Org, "Women in the Workplace 2019," October 15, 2019, womenintheworkplace.com/.

Rule #1: Call Her by Her Name

1. Philip Landau, "Discrimination at work: honey, I just got sued," *Guardian,* April 26, 2012, www.theguardian.com/money/work-blog/2012/apr/26/discrimination-work -terms-of-endearment.

2. Landau, "Discrimination at work: honey, I just got sued."

3. Dan Harris, "Obama's 'Sweetie': Spontaneous or Sexist?" ABC News, May 16, 2008, abcnews.go.com/GMA/Vote2008/story?id=4870599.

4   Justin Wolfers, "Fewer Women Run Big Companies Than Men Named John," *New York Times*, The Upshot (newsletter), March 2, 2015, https://www.nytimes.com/2015/03/03/upshot/fewer-women-run-big-companies-than-men-named-john.html.

5   Julia A. Files, Anita P. Mayer, Marcia G. Ko, et al., "Speaker Introductions at Internal Medicine Grand Rounds: Forms of Address Reveal Gender Bias," *Journal of Women's Health* 26, no. 5 (May 1, 2017): 413–19, doi.org/10.1089/jwh.2016.6044.

6   Stav Atir and Melissa J Ferguson, "How gender determines the way we speak about professionals," *Proceedings of the National Academy of Sciences of the United States of America* 115, no. 28 (July 10, 2018): 7278–83, doi.org/10.1073/pnas.1805284115.

7   Clare McLaughlin, "The Lasting Impact of Mispronouncing Students' Names," neaToday, September 1, 2016, neatoday.org/2016/09/01/pronouncing-students-names/.

8   McLaughlin, "The Lasting Impact of Mispronouncing Students' Names."

9   Jessica Valenti, "Men who use nicknames for women to win fights are creepy, sexist and dumb," *Guardian*, April 28, 2014, www.theguardian.com/commentisfree/2014/apr/28/men-nicknames-for-women-sexist.

10   Scottie Andrew, "Men More Likely to Be Known by Surname Than Women, a Sign of Gender Bias, Researchers Say," *Newsweek*, June 26, 2018, www.newsweek.com/men-more-likely-be-called-last-name-sign-bias-995024.

11   Linda B. Glaser, "When last comes first: the gender bias of names," *Cornell Chronicle*, July 2, 2018, news.cornell.edu/stories/2018/07/when-last-comes-first-gender-bias-names.

12   Glaser, "When last comes first: the gender bias of names."

13   Atir and Ferguson, "How gender determines the way we speak about professionals."

14   Claire Cain Miller and Derek Willis, "Maiden Names: On the Rise Again," *New York Times*, The Upshot (newsletter), June 27, 2015, www.nytimes.com/2015/06/28/upshot/maiden-names-on-the-rise-again.html.

15   Amanda Marcotte, "Women Who Take Their Husband's Name Perceived as Less Competent but More Caring," *Slate*, January 17, 2014, slate.com/human-interest/2014/01/corrected-another-reason-to-keep-your-name-when-getting-married-better-job-offers.html.

Rule #2: Be Someone She Can Relate To

1   DiSC Profile, "DiSC Overview," accessed June 5, 2020, www.discprofile.com/what-is-disc/overview/.

Rule #3: Don't Ask, "What Does Your Husband Do?"

1   Selena Coppock, Twitter post, May 7, 2015, 9:49 AM, twitter.com/NYTvows/status/596310972198957057; Selena Coppock, Twitter post, August 9, 2015, 1:21 PM, twitter.com/NYTvows/status/630428750228914176.

2   Philip Cohen, "Women's Employment and the Decline in Marriage Are No Longer Related," *Atlantic*, April 16, 2013, www.theatlantic.com/sexes/archive/2013/04/womens-employment-and-the-decline-in-marriage-are-no-longer-related/275009/.

3   Bryan Caplan, "What Is the Female Marriage Penalty?" EconLog, February 29, 2012, www.econlib.org/archives/2012/02/what_is_the_fem.html; Bryan Caplan, "What Is the Male Marriage Premium?" EconLog, February 28, 2012, www.econlib.org/archives/2012/02/what_is_the_mar.html.

4   Diana Bruk, "20 Percent of All Weddings Are Called Off—Here's Why," Best Life Online, May 15, 2018, https://bestlifeonline.com/engagements-called-off-break-up-stories/.

5   Maddy Sims, "Here's the Average Length of Engagement for Couples," *The Knot* (blog), www.theknot.com/content/too-long-to-be-engaged; Abigail Tracy and Matan Gilat, "Married Couples in This State Wait the Longest to Have a Baby," Vocativ, April 29, 2015, www.vocativ.com/188018/married-couples-in-this-state-wait-the-longest-to-have-a-baby/index.html.

6   "Employee Tenure in 2018," Bureau of Labor Statistics, September 20, 2018, www.bls.gov/news.release/tenure.nr0.htm.

7   Alicia Vanorman and Linda A. Jacobsen, "U.S. Household Composition Shifts as the Population Grows Older; More Young Adults Live with Parents," PRB, February 12, 2020, www.prb.org/u-s-household-composition-shifts-as-the-population-grows-older-more-young-adults-live-with-parents/.

8   "ForbesWoman, TheKnot & WeddingChannel.com: The Work & Wedding Survey," *The Knot* (blog), accessed June 5, 2020, https://www.theknot.com/content/the-knot-forbeswoman-survey-results.

9   "Life and Leadership After HBS," Harvard Business School, May 2015, www.hbs.edu/women50/docs/L_and_L_Survey_2Findings_12final.pdf.

Rule #4: Don't Sit in Her Chair

1   Lynda Laughlin, "Maternity Leave and Employment Patterns of First-Time Mothers: 1961–2008," United States Census Bureau, October 2011, www.census.gov/prod/2011pubs/p70-128.pdf.

2   Laughlin, "Maternity Leave and Employment Patterns of First-Time Mothers: 1961–2008."

3   "What the Law Says About Breastfeeding and Work," US Department of Health and Human Services, Office on Women's Health, accessed June 5, 2020, www.womenshealth.gov/supporting-nursing-moms-work/what-law-says-about-breastfeeding-and-work.

4   Amanda Macmillan, "Maternity Leave Isn't Getting More Popular," *Time*, January 19, 2017, time.com/4639269/maternity-leave-rates/.

5   Stephen Miller, "Common Paid Leave Practices Could Be Reinforcing Gender Roles,
     Survey Suggests," *Society for Human Resource Management,* October 6, 2016, www
     .shrm.org/resourcesandtools/hr-topics/benefits/pages/shrm-survey-paid-leave.

6   Maggie Overfelt, "Paternity Leave 101: What to Know About Taking Time Off," The
     Bump, July 2019, www.thebump.com/a/paternity-leave-for-men.

7   Susan Scutti, "The Average American Dad Is Getting Older, Study Finds," CNN,
     August 30, 2017, www.cnn.com/2017/08/30/health/older-dads-us-study/index.html;
     Quoctrung Bui and Claire Cain Miller, "The Age That Women Have Babies: How a Gap
     Divides America," *New York Times,* August 4, 2018, www.nytimes.com/interactive
     /2018/08/04/upshot/up-birth-age-gap.html.

8   Kristi Hedges, "Five Reasons We're Losing a Whole Generation of Managers," *Forbes,*
     January 16, 2013, www.forbes.com/sites/work-in-progress/2013/01/16/five-reasons
     -were-losing-a-whole-generation-of-managers/#cd9749613a0f.

9   Madeline Buxton, "Stitch Fix CEO Katrina Lake Talks About Leading a Public Com-
     pany & Her Upcoming Maternity Leave," Refinery29, June 18, 2018, www.refinery29
     .com/en-us/2018/06/202050/katrina-lake-stitch-fix-amazon-maternity-leave.

10   "Facebook's Mark Zuckerberg to Take 2 Months of Paternity Leave," Reuters, August
     18, 2017, www.businessinsider.com/r-facebooks-mark-zuckerberg-to-take-2-months
     -of-paternity-leave-2017-8.

Rule #5: Watch the Clock

1   ThriveAP, "Here's How to React If Your Boss Changes Your Schedule," December 11,
     2018, thriveap.com/blog/heres-how-react-if-your-boss-changes-your-schedule.

2   Claire Cain Miller, "Men Do More at Home, but Not as Much as They Think They Do,"
     New York Times, The Upshot (newsletter), November 12, 2015, www.nytimes.com/2015
     /11/12/upshot/men-do-more-at-home-but-not-as-much-as-they-think-they-do.html.

3   Jeff Grabmeier, "Gender Gap in Parenting, Housework Remains Wide," Ohio State Uni-
     versity College of Education and Human Ecology, October 9, 2017, ehe.osu.edu/news
     /listing/gender-gap-parenting-housework-remains-wide/.

4   "Time Spent in Leisure Activities in 2014, by Gender, Age, and Educational Attain-
     ment," US Bureau of Labor Statistics, June 29, 2015, www.bls.gov/opub/ted/2015/time
     -spent-in-leisure-activities-in-2014-by-gender-age-and-educational-attainment.htm.

5   Chabeli Carrazana, "America's First Female Recession," *The 19th,* August 2, 2020,
     19thnews.org/2020/08/americas-first-female-recession/.

6   Caitlyn Collins, Liana Christin Landivar, Leah Ruppanner, and William J. Scarborough,
     "COVID-19 and the Gender Gap in Work Hours," *Gender, Work & Organization,* June
     27, 2020, doi.org/10.1111/gwao.12506.

7   Julien Laloyaux, Frank Laroi, and Marco Hirnstein, "Women and Men Are Equally Bad at Multitasking," *Harvard Business Review*, September 26, 2018, hbr.org/2018/09/research-women-and-men-are-equally-bad-at-multitasking.

8   Leah Ruppanner, "Women Are Not Better at Multitasking. They Just Do More Work, Studies Show," August 15, 2019, Science Alert, www.sciencealert.com/women-aren-t-better-multitaskers-than-men-they-re-just-doing-more-work; James Morgan, "Women 'Better at Multitasking' Than Men, Study Finds," October 24, 2013, BBC News, https://www.bbc.com/news/science-environment-24645100.

Rule #6: Speak Up So That She Doesn't Have To

1   Kerri Anne Renzulli, "Almost Half of Men Say They Don't Know What's an Acceptable Compliment to Give a Coworker," CNBC, March 13, 2019, www.cnbc.com/2019/03/13/46percent-of-men-dont-know-whats-an-acceptable-compliment-to-give-at-work.html.

2   Sangeeta Badal, "The Business Benefits of Gender Diversity," January 20, 2014, www.gallup.com/workplace/236543/business-benefits-gender-diversity.aspx.

3   Stephen Turban, Dan Wu, and Letian (LT) Zhang, "Research: When Gender Diversity Makes Firms More Productive," *Harvard Business Review*, February 11, 2019, hbr.org/2019/02/research-when-gender-diversity-makes-firms-more-productive.

4   Malli Gero and Stephanie Sonnabend, "2020 Women on Boards Gender Diversity Index," 2020 Women on Boards, 2015, 2020wob.com/wp-content/uploads/2019/09/2020GDI-2015Report.pdf.

5   Lois Joy, Harvey M. Wagner, and Sriram Narayanan, "The Bottom Line: Corporate Performance and Women's Representation on Boards," Catalyst.org, October 15, 2007, www.catalyst.org/research/the-bottom-line-corporate-performance-and-womens-representation-on-boards/.

6   V.W. Kramer, A.M. Konrad, and S. Erkut, "Critical Mass on Corporate Boards: Why Three or More Women Enhance Governance," Wellesley Center for Women's Publications, 2006, www.wcwonline.org/Publications-by-title/critical-mass-on-corporate-boards-why-three-or-more-women-enhance-governance-executive-summary.

7   Julie C. Norris, "Women on Boards: Review and Outlook," The Conference Board, May 2012, www.ced.org/pdf/DN-V4N9-12_Women_on_Boards_-_Review_and_Outlook.pdf.

8   "Every Other One," Committee for Economic Development, Policy Brief, November 14, 2016, www.ced.org/reports/every-other-one-a-status-update.

Rule #7: Don't Make Her Ask Twice

1   Amy Elisa Jackson, "New Study: Job Seekers Expect Salary Negotiation & Transparency," April 10, 2019, www.glassdoor.com/employers/blog/job-seekers-expect-salary-negotiation-transparency/.

2   Hannah Riley Bowles, Linda Babcock, and Lei Lai, "Social Incentives for Gender Differences in the Propensity to Initiate Negotiations: Sometimes It Does Hurt to Ask," *Organizational Behavior and Human Decision Processes* 103 (November 7, 2006), www.cfa.harvard.edu/cfawis/bowles.pdf.

3   Ryan Golden, "Match Group Accounts 100% Pay Equity Following Audit," *HR Dive*, December 18, 2018, https://www.hrdive.com/news/match-group-announces-100-pay -equity-following-audit/544621/.

Rule #8: Be an Equal Opportunity Asshole

1   Melody Wilding, "The Surprising Truth About Crying at Work," *Forbes*, June 11, 2018, www.forbes.com/sites/melodywilding/2018/06/11/the-surprising-truth-about-crying -at-work/#12d0277d4e79; Tim Herrera, "Why You Shouldn't Feel Bad About Crying at Work," *New York Times* Smarter Living (newsletter), October 14, 2018, www.nytimes .com/2018/10/14/smarter-living/crying-at-work.html.

2   Herrera, "Why You Shouldn't Feel Bad About Crying at Work."

3   Lindsay Lavine, "Why Women Fail to Speak Up at High-Level Meetings and What Everyone Can Do About It," *Fast Company*, May 21, 2014, www.fastcompany.com /3030861/why-women-fail-to-speak-up-at-high-level-meetings-and-what-everyone -can-do-about.

4   Leah E. White, "Gender as a Predictor of Competitive Success in Extemporaneous Speaking," *National Forensic Journal*, Spring 1997, pdfs.semanticscholar.org/b1d7 /c545e5ab42a4644d657aac73408836297d8f.pdf.

5   Kaitlyn Mitchell, "We Crunched the Numbers on How Much Stage Time Female Comedians Get," Bitch Media, February 4, 2015, www.bitchmedia.org/post/we -crunched-the-numbers-on-how-much-stagetime-female-comedians-get.

6   Chris C. Gernreich and Christina Exner," A Comparison of the Influence of Gender on Managerial Decision Making," ResearchGate, June 2015, www.researchgate.net /publication/278679030_A_Comparison_of_the_Influence_of_Gender_on_Managerial _Decision_Making.

7   Benjamin Haimowitz, "Women Greatly Underrate Their Standing with Bosses and Other Workers, Study Finds," Academy of Management, July 1, 2009, aom.org/News/ Press-Releases/Women-greatly-underrate-their-standing-with-bosses-and-other -workers,-study-finds.aspx.

8   Felix Richter, "Women Still Underrepresented in Tech," Statista, February 19, 2020, www.statista.com/chart/4467/female-employees-at-tech-companies/.

9   Nicole Gugliucci, Twitter post, September 22, 2017, 9:01AM, twitter.com /noisyastronomer/status/911213826527436800?lang=en.

Rule #9: Tell Her That You See Her Potential

1   Tara Sophia Mohr, "Why Women Don't Apply for Jobs Unless They're 100% Qualified," *Harvard Business Review*, August 25, 2014, hbr.org/2014/08/why-women-dont-apply -for-jobs-unless-theyre-100-qualified.

2   Mohr, "Why Women Don't Apply for Jobs Unless They're 100% Qualified."

3   Laura Guillén, Margarita Mayo, and Natalia Karelaia, "Appearing Self-Confident and Getting Credit for It: Why It May Be Easier for Men Than Women to Gain Influence at Work," *Human Resource Management* 57, no. 4 (July/August 2018): 839–54, doi.org/10 .1002/hrm.21857.

4   Laura Guillén, "Is the Confidence Gap Between Men and Women a Myth?" *Harvard Business Review,* March 26, 2018, hbr.org/2018/03/is-the-confidence-gap-between -men-and-women-a-myth.

5   David M. Mayer, "How Not to Advocate for a Woman at Work," *Harvard Business Review,* July 26, 2017, hbr.org/2017/07/how-not-to-advocate-for-a-woman-at-work.

Conclusion

1   Emma Hinchliffe, "GM's Board Will Have More Women Than Men. It's Not the Only One," *Fortune,* May 20, 2019, fortune.com/2019/05/20/women-boards-fortune-500 -2019/.

2   Lizette Chapman and Bloomberg, "Venture Capital, Long a Boy's Club, Makes Some Progress in Adding Women," *Fortune,* February 7, 2020, fortune.com/2020/02/07 /venture-capital-women-diversity/.

3   Dominic-Madori Davis, "Meet the Only 4 Black Fortune 500 CEOs," *Business Insider*, February 28, 2020, www.businessinsider.com/there-are-four-black-fortune-500-ceos -here-they-are-2020-2.

4   Kate Clark, "81% of VC Firms Don't Have a Single Black Investor—BLCK VC Wants to Change That," *TechCrunch*, November 8, 2018, techcrunch.com/2018/11/08/81-of-vc -firms-dont-have-a-single-black-investor-blck-vc-plans-on-changing-that/.

INDEX

ABOUT THE AUTHOR

Photo by Chris Taggart

Kate Eberle Walker is the CEO of PresenceLearning, the leading provider of online special education services for K–12 schools. In this role, she leads a majority-female employee population in their mission to provide a flexible career path for over more than thousand special education therapists, most of whom are working mothers.

Kate worked her way up to become CEO of The Princeton Review in 2015 at age thirty-nine. While CEO, she not only made the business profitable, she did so while building a 50 percent female executive team, having tasked herself with the goal of making her C-suite fully aligned with the gender balance of the organization as a whole. She offers straight, tell-it-like-it-is advice to her fellow CEOs, especially men, and serves as a behind-the-scenes advisor to many of them, who genuinely want to know how to do a better job of managing women. She is known as an approachable and relatable mentor to younger women, whom she regularly supports and advises on career decisions.

Before becoming a CEO, Kate navigated the male-dominated world of Wall Street as a Goldman Sachs investment banker for five years straight out of college. Then, after getting her MBA at Harvard Business School, she went on to lead the mergers and acquisitions team at Kaplan, a global education company, for nearly ten years.

Kate is an active advisor, mentor, and board member to many education-focused teams and organizations. She serves as a board member for Rosetta Stone (a language and literacy learning company), Prospect Schools (a charter school management organization), and the International School of Brooklyn (a private K–8 school). She represents and advocates for diverse representation in companies and on boards.

She lives in Brooklyn with her husband, Chris, and their two daughters, Marion and Audrey.